A UNIQUE SOCIETY

A

UNIQUE

SOCIETY

a history of

The Salvation Army

Assurance Society Limited

by BERNARD WATSON

© THE SALVATION ARMY 1968

First published in 1968
by Salvationist Publishing & Supplies, Ltd.,
Judd Street, King's Cross,
London, W.C.1.

SBN 85412 001 7

Lieut.-Colonel Bernard Watson has been a Salvation Army officer since 1926. After serving as a corps officer in Great Britain he came to the Editorial Department at International Headquarters in 1936. He is the founder-editor of *Vanguard*.

Made and printed in Great Britain
in Garamond type by
The Campfield Press, St. Albans, Herts.

From the Memorandum of Association

of

The Salvation Army Assurance
Society Limited

The objects for which the Society is established are:

- (*a*) To promote and support the religious and other charitable work of The Salvation Army;
- (*b*) To undertake and carry on life assurance business of every description;
- (*c*) To do all such other things as are incidental or conducive to the aforesaid objects or either of them.

CONTENTS

ILLUSTRATIONS

FOREWORD

WHETHER any preface ever helped to sell a book is a moot point. This one really needs no such adventitious puff—and that for two reasons.

One is the author's own skill, long acknowledged by those who know him best and have read him most. His lively pen holds our interest throughout. The reader may think that he is giving attention to these pages; in reality these pages are holding his attention.

The second is that the story of The Salvation Army Assurance Society is a success story. Incredible to think that at one time a virulent press paragraph could allege that, when a claim was made, the Army had to mount the drum at the street corner in order to meet it.

In one sense these two aspects of our work are separate. The Society's ability to meet every just claim has long been acknowledged on every hand. But in another sense they are indivisible, for the officers and staff of the Society are numbered among our most ardent Salvationists.

Long may they continue to be such, and long may the Society continue to flourish—for the benefit of the policy-holders and the furtherance of the work of The Salvation Army.

FREDERICK COUTTS,
General.

Chapter One

HOW IT BEGAN

W HEN, in 1891, The Salvation Army acquired the Methodist and General Assurance Society the new times had arrived, the modern times. The great reform acts were in being; primary education for all children was in force; Dickens was dead; the telephone and the Daimler car had arrived; Darwin had shaken the theological confidence of many churchmen. Life-expectancy was increasing; infant mortality declining. The population of the United Kingdom had reached 33,000,000. Edwin Chadwick had created a conscience about public health; Joseph Chamberlain, as Lord Mayor of Birmingham, had pushed through slum clearance schemes, with municipal gas, water and sanitation services.

These blessings had been known for some time but Chamberlain gave them to the labouring classes. That was new. The working man was somebody in England. He had a vote and, more important, pennies and even shillings to spend. It was the emergence of the working class as a major economic force that brought into being industrial life assurance.

The worker was even learning about thrift, joining friendly societies, using the Post Office Savings Bank. Some daring spirits had grasped the astonishing idea that a labouring man could buy his own house. On thirty shillings a week he could be passing rich and many workers now earned that sum and more.

So 1891 was a good time to enter the perilous field of life assurance. Admittedly, The Salvation Army issued no policies until 1894, but the wish was there from the first. Caution was the watchword. Recent history was strewn with the wreckage of mushroom societies. Others eked out a precarious existence, sometimes hanging on with the aid of dubious or illegal practices. The Chief of the Staff,

Bramwell Booth, the dominant figure on the board of the infant Society, knew little about life assurance, and until he did would not be talked into precipitate action. The first ordinary branch policy was issued January 1, 1894. It was on the life of Major Ernest A. Bremner, the Army's Property Secretary and a leading figure in the negotiations for the transfer of the Society. He was the first Managing Director of the Society. The first industrial branch policy was issued in March the same year.

One man, more than any other, deserves mention in the history of the transfer of the Methodist and General to The Salvation Army. James Field was for some time Corps Sergeant-Major at Clapton Congress Hall. An expert in life assurance, he was on the board of the Methodist and General and knew that it was in serious difficulties. It had been hard hit by an adverse court decision at Wednesbury and brought near to disaster by a badly managed sick-benefit scheme. Excessive claims by malingerers, and poor local supervision, proved to be ruinous.

Harder for the disappointed management and guarantors to understand was the failure of Methodists to use the Society for their own assurances. In 1867, when the Methodist and General began, it was frequently the case that premiums had to be paid in a public house. Total abstinence was a live issue in the Methodist Church of that time. So to guard against temptation the policy-holders were offered teetotal facilities. But all in vain. At the time when the Methodist board threw in its hand there were only 450 policies and £800 liabilities.

In Birmingham, the Abstainers and General Assurance Company had been negotiating for the take-over of the Methodist and General. This concern did in fact accept the transfer of the policies but Salvationist James Field approached the Army, arousing the interest of the Chief of the Staff, Bramwell Booth, in the possibility of acquiring the all-important charter.

First discussions took place in the home of young Major David Lamb, at Kenmure Road, Hackney. He was attached

to The Salvation Army's Property Department, in which
Major Ernest Bremner was in charge of the preliminary
negotiations. It may have seemed proper to put the new
venture in the care of the property men because it was

No. 3596 c.

Certificate of Change of Name

OF THE

Methodist and General Assurance Society Limited

I hereby Certify, That the

Methodist and General Assurance Society Limited

having, with the sanction of a **Special Resolution** of the said Company, and with the approval of the BOARD OF TRADE, changed its name, is now called the

Salvation Army Assurance Society, Limited

and I have entered such new name on the Register accordingly.

Given under my hand at London, this *Eighteenth* day of *April* One Thousand Nine Hundred and *four*

Registrar of Joint Stock Companies.

hoped that a function of the Society would be to provide
mortgages on properties for corps in the rapidly expanding
British Territory. In fact, among the first advances from

the Society's funds were mortgages on Salvation Army halls, more than £6,000 by the end of 1891, which was not a full year's working.

For the first thirteen years of its assurance venture The Salvation Army had to accept a most unwieldy name. There were one or two variations but for the most part the title used until the Registrar gave permission for the change, in 1904, was *Salvation Army Life Assurance in connexion with the Methodist and General Assurance Society, Limited.*

Chapter Two

LIFE ASSURANCE
AS A GAMBLE

THE fact that Methodists or Salvationists could be associated with life assurance was proof that it had come a long way from dubiety to respectability, and this for the most part in William Booth's lifetime. In his father's day it had been a gamble. No ' insurable interest ' was required. The life of Robert Walpole was insured for thousands of pounds by people who hoped to profit by his early death. When George II went to fight at Drettingen premiums were five shillings in the pound against his return. He was not a popular king and perhaps those who took out a policy hoped that he would die in battle. However, he returned from the war unrepentant and unreformed.

Admiral Byng, shot for cowardice, most unjustly, proved to be an irresistible magnet for speculative insurers. This, and even the continuance in favour of a king's mistresses, was considered suitable for the issuing of policies.

There was little respect for the science of life assurance, probably because little existed. The reliability of the actuary, whose calculations were fundamental to sound insurance, was held in contempt. Addison, of *The Spectator*, composed a ' bill of mortality ' which mocked the mortality tables of his day:

> Tim Tattle killed by the tap of a fan on his left shoulder by Coquetilla, as he talked carelessly with her at a bow-window.
> Samuel Felt, haberdasher, wounded in his walks to Islington by Mrs. Susanna Cross-Stitch, as she was clambering over a stile.
> John Pleadwell, Esq., of the Middle Temple, assassinated in his chambers, the 6th instant, by Kitty Sly, who pretended to come to him for advice.

Another wag was sarcastic:

Of a six-bar gate	. . . . . .	4
Of a quick-set hedge	. . . . .	2
Broke his neck in robbing a hen roost	. . .	1
Surfeit of curds and cream	. . . . .	2

Yet insurance had a long and respectable history going back to Roman times. The British Parliament enacted its first statute on 'assurance' in 1601. The earliest known life-policy was effected in 1583. But by the time Dickens began to paint his vivid word pictures of England, in the 1840s, the modern concept of life assurance was beginning to emerge. Of course there were still black sheep. The frauds depicted in *Martin Chuzzlewit* were based on fact:

> 'I take it all myself,' said Tigg Montague. 'Here I am responsible for everything. The only responsible person in the establishment! Ha, ha, ha! Then there are the life assurances without loans: the common policies. Very profitable, very comfortable. Money down, you know; repeated every year; capital fun!'
>
> 'But when they begin to fall in,' observed Jonas. 'It's all very well, while the office is young, but when the policies begin to die; that's what I am thinking of.'
>
> 'At the first start, my dear fellow,' said Montague, 'to show you how correct your judgment is, we had a couple of unlucky deaths that brought us down to a grand piano.'
>
> 'Brought you down where?' cried Jonas.
>
> 'I give you my sacred word of honour,' said Tigg Montague, 'that I raised money on every other individual piece of property, and was left alone in the world with a grand piano. And it was an upright-grand too, so that I couldn't even sit upon it. But, my dear fellow, we got over it. We granted many new policies that week (liberal allowances to solicitors, by-the-by), and got over it in no time. Whenever they should chance to fall in heavily, as you very justly observe they may, one of these days; then—' he finished the sentence in so low a whisper, that only one disconnected word was audible, and that imperfectly. But it sounded like 'Bolt'.
>
> 'Why, you're as bold as brass!' said Jonas, in the utmost admiration.
>
> 'A man can well afford to be as bold as brass, my good fellow, when he gets gold in exchange!' cried the chairman, with a laugh that shook him from head to foot.

While Dickens was writing his book, William Booth was twelve years of age and learning fast. A Parliamentary Committee was sitting to 'examine the fraudulent promotion of companies'. Mr. Gladstone, who came to have grave doubts about life assurance, was the chairman. And while Booth read and remembered, Dickens wrote the popularized, dramatized and somewhat exaggerated account in *Martin Chuzzlewit*. The bogus company was the West Middlesex General Annuity Assurance Company* (the actual frauds of which were revealed to Mr. Gladstone's committee) to become in Dickens's novel the Anglo-Bengalee Disinterested Loan and Life Assurance Company. Tigg Montague was the villain and he ' chose a life assurance company because large sums could be collected as premiums for life assurance or annuities with no legal obligation to reserve the amounts required for the future obligations on the death of the assured or the survival of the annuitant '.

Of course, The Salvation Army was of itself the guarantee of the strength of the new Society. There was no £20,000 deposit and no well-to-do shareholders. Normally large capital resources are required to sustain a new society in its first ten years of life. The Legal and General was launched with an issue of 20,000 shares at £50 each, an initial fund of one million pounds—a typical beginning for a new life office. But Salvation Army assurance had to content itself with building up its resources slowly, relying largely on the religion and good sense of its agents. Twenty years elapsed before The Salvation Army, as the proprietors, took the first profit, the sum of £6,768, in 1911. Since then The Salvation Army has received annual and increasing amounts from the Society.

By the end of 1897 total funds were £28,254, of which The Salvation Army had contributed £24,000 to enable it ' to keep the society entirely in its own hands both in control and profit '. The premium income for that year was £41,376 3s. 6d., over £35,000 of which was industrial branch.

* From the Introduction to *Martin Chuzzlewit*, Oxford University Press, 1951, by Geoffrey Russell.

Chapter Three

THE BACKGROUND

WILLIAM BOOTH thought of life assurance as a social service and at its best, of course, that is what it is. Though the Founder was not the first to see it in that light few men knew the poor more intimately than he. The pawnshop had been his high-school; the Methodist chapel his university. When he completed his apprenticeship and set out for London, in 1849, he already carried in his mind, and on his heart, a knowledge of the plight of the working classes and a vision of their succour both on earth and in heaven. He was familiar with the fears and superstitions of the illiterate mining and factory workers of England.

He knew what they felt about funerals. His own father had died a bankrupt leaving his family in poverty. The cost of burial had been a strain on the meagre family resources; it was always the most ruinously expensive item in a Victorian budget.

Booth knew about the paupers' graves which filled the cemeteries at Nottingham to overflowing:

> The grave was fifteen or twenty feet deep, with the bodies put in one upon another. There will be about eight adult persons in the grave and they will finish off the top with a layer of four children. There may be twelve to sixteen people in the grave.

In *The American Way of Death*, by Jessica Mitford, mention is made of the bargaining power of British undertakers and a mid-nineteenth century report on the subject of burial costs and practices by Sir Edwin Chadwick:

> The circumstances of the death do not admit of any effective competition or any precedent examination of the charges of different undertakers, or any comparison and consideration of their supplies; there is no time to change them for others that are less expensive. . . . If there be any sort of service in which principles of civil policy and motives of ordinary benevolence and charity, require to be placed under public regulation, for the protection of the private individual who is helpless, it is surely this, at the time of extreme misery.

It is still possible to find grief-stricken and not well-off people at this great disadvantage, as Miss Mitford's book and Evelyn Waugh's *The Loved One* show. Miss Mitford quotes a funeral service journal:

> A funeral is not an occasion for a display of cheapness. It is, in fact, an opportunity for the display of a status symbol which, by bolstering family pride, does much to assuage grief. A funeral is also an occasion when feelings of guilt and remorse are satisfied to a large extent by the purchase of a fine funeral. It seems highly probable that the most satisfactory funeral service for the average family is one in which the cost has necessitated some degree of sacrifice. This permits the survivors to atone for any real or fancied neglect of the deceased prior to his death.

William Booth, one of whose first essays in social work, as a youth, had been the attempt to give decent burial to an old abandoned woman, was aware of the feelings of working-class mothers. They regarded a pauper's funeral as a public humiliation, and shrank from it with dread. No sacrifice was too great in order to prevent such a stigma and this made such women ready clients not only of the majority of honest collecting societies and burial clubs but also prey for those who were ready like vultures at the kill to make profit out of death.

High-pressure canvassing was rife, lapses were welcomed, notices of arrears were not sent. Many a fearful woman would undertake to pay what she could not afford, only to lose all her premiums during one of the frequent periods of bad trade. Then in the ever-recurring epidemics of typhoid, cholera, diphtheria or influenza, the mortality rate for children would rise steeply. When William Booth was living in Camberwell, London, in 1849 about 200 children died in an orphanage in nearby Clapham during a cholera outbreak.

So he knew the fears of the poor and he also had personal experience of the security provided by life assurance. He once failed a medical examination for life cover, though later a number of pessimistic verdicts on his health by doctors were shown to have been unfounded. But he took care to give his family protection.

'We shall want £21 for assurance directly,' he wrote home to Catherine from Sheffield, in 1864. For him that was a large sum. William Booth was always a poor man and the date of the letter shows it to be the period when he was 'in the wilderness', having resigned his charge in Newcastle upon Tyne and having found, as yet, no other. £21 in a lump sum indicates ordinary branch assurance, the yearly, half-yearly, or quarterly payment preferred by the thrifty, businesslike middle classes—the wealthy, upper-class man had little or no recourse to life assurance. He had no need.

But at the other end of the scale the poorest, the self-respecting working man was becoming assurance minded, encouraged as he was, pressurized by the fast-growing, enormous life offices.

Whether or not the working man believed all the claims made for life assurance by the growing volume of assurance advertising, one thing he did know, that 'Death is common, and all that live must die' as Shakespeare put it.

The copy-writer of one society put these words into the mouth of a working man:

> I joined them many years ago,
>   And ne'er had cause to rue.
> At first I had a penny,
>   Which I soon increased to two.
> But now I pay in threepence,
>   And the claim is eighteen pounds.
> Will it not be a nice round sum,
>   To lay me in the ground?

For many a coal-miner in South Wales, the Midlands, the North East, and Scotland for whom, in those days, sudden death was a constant companion, those few pennies a week provided the wherewithal for new suits and dresses for the family. All in black, they would walk behind his coffin. It would be a good coffin, with a hearse, and a knife-and-fork tea to follow. It had to be a decent funeral; this was a deep primeval urge. It had been felt by countless generations, from prehistoric times, when early man found himself awed by the mystery of death, and laid food, drinking cup and sword in the grave for the last journey of the departed. A Saxon chieftain, buried at Hoo, in East Anglia, was left with his boats, his golden helmets, his shield and his axe—well equipped for his triumphant voyage to Valhalla. Pharaohs were entombed in mighty pyramids, their slain servants about them, their men at arms and cattle to protect them and give sustenance for their journey into the darkness.

Down the centuries, and influenced in some degree by Christianity, burial became for the ordinary man a preacher, flowers, new clothes and the singing of hymns—the nineteenth-century equivalents of ancient burial customs. A man spent more on his funeral than upon his wedding and that was where the life assurance policy came in. Those who had long since ceased attending chapel none the less expected and received a Christian burial.

To some this gave a brief moment of drama and prominence. Those who had been inarticulate, obscure, who had never been the recipients of public attention while they lived, had it now as the polished coffin, decked with wreaths, and gleaming name plate, was carried to the place prepared for it, while relatives and friends walked before and behind.

Of such it might be said, as of the Thane of Cawdor, in *Macbeth*, 'Nothing in his life became him like the leaving it.'

Chapter Four

THE MAN ON
THE DOORSTEP

THE agent was the man on whom William Booth based his hopes for the future of Salvationist life assurance. He became a familiar figure on the doorstep of thousands of homes. First, he gained admittance and then the confidence of the householders. He had to reduce life assurance to simple human proportions. In what he called his ' Ordination Address ' to agents the Founder said (see page 55):

> The Salvation Army Life Assurance Society is a very important organization, and that because, among other things, of the greatness of the principles for which it exists—that is, to bless and save the souls and bodies of men, and to make them in turn saviours of those about them.
>
> You may imagine yourself to be on a lower level than the ordinary spiritual officer. You may even be regarded as being lower by those who do not understand you, and you may be more than taken up with one particular way of doing things, but the object is the same. Your work is the same as mine; we are both aiming at the same thing. You reach the goal one way, I another. . . .
>
> We want to raise up a body of men not only able to do this assurance work, but able to turn their hands to anything else. Yours is a great opportunity because, as you go along, you will become more and more known. Your name will become known. . . . The assurance agent goes in and out. He does not go in to beg, but holds his head up, and goes in with his book in hand as a public benefactor. . . .
>
> In and out, threading his way, the assurance agent goes. One agent said he paid five hundred visits a week; he made his book, and all the while he was promoting the cause of The Salvation Army. They will say of such a man, ' He does not come after our souls only; he has come to do us good with our bodies, and help our little children.' . . .
>
> You have got a way of getting in without any scraping or toadying, and looking as if you were earning a living out of religion. The more you realize you are a public benefactor, the more the people will believe you are one. They will take you at your own estimate. No whining about being a poor unworthy brother who has had to take to assurance as a last resource! . . .
>
> There has never been anybody else who has adopted such a thing. Assurance agencies and companies have made a great deal of money, but nobody has gone with the simple motive of saving

the souls of the people, and using the profit that is made to the shaking of the foundations of the Wicked One. . . .

I don't want any business founded on falsehood—God forbid! Buttresses and foundations that are built upon falsehood will totter and fall. We want men and women who are true—who would scorn to tell a lie. The agents of this Society should be able to look God in the face and say, ' I never tell a lie in my books, in my report to the Society, in my representations of the Society, or lie in my reckonings. I am true and honest—true in everything through and through!' We want truth—liars are not God's agents. If anybody here has got an unconfessed, unpardoned lie upon his conscience he ought to get it washed away by the Blood of the Lamb. Where are you now? We ought to part, every man of us, with a blue sky. If you will do this, what a wonderful future there is before you! You will have your troubles and trials, but you have friends behind you and before you! Now, then, come along; make a clear fresh start here and now. Are you right with God? Is there anyone here who wants a clean heart, who is willing to pay the price? If so God will give it to you now!

In seeing the need for such men as an indispensable part of his life assurance venture the Founder was wiser than that fount of wisdom Mr. William Ewart Gladstone, the great Liberal statesman. As Chancellor of the Exchequer Gladstone became interested in the large life assurance interests in the City, and in many provincial centres, where they were growing apace. Probably the most brilliant and hard-working chancellor in British history, Gladstone soon had a firm grasp of life assurance practices. Some of his speeches in the House of Commons reveal understanding of its complexities that has never been surpassed by a politician.

Gladstone soon developed strong objections both to the cost and methods of door-to-door agency collecting. He came to the opinion that undue pressure was often exerted and that a high percentage of lapses were a result. He told the House of Commons:

The Friends of Need Society in five years had 18,000 lapses of 86,000 policies issued—18,000 people who had insured their lives and lost the whole benefit of their money!

Indignant at what he considered to be unnecessary duplication of collections and dubious methods of some collectors, Gladstone persuaded a reluctant Parliament to go into life assurance in competition with the life offices. Premiums were to be paid over Post Office counters and the administration of the scheme, with unconscious irony as it proved, was placed in the hands of the Commissioners for the National Debt.

From the first, unlike most schemes of this great man, Gladstone's ' do it yourself ' life assurance was a fiasco. In seventeen years, with the whole resources of the Post Office behind the scheme, only 6,500 policies were taken out, whereas at the end of its first four years Salvation Army assurance had 122,339 policies in force. This was a rate of progress which, if they heard of it, must have made Mr. Gladstone and his Post Office experts ponder ruefully on the vagaries of a business in which a lot of religious amateurs could make a host of professional experts seem to be ridiculous.

Mr. Gladstone lacked William Booth's knowledge of the psychology of the working class. The Liberal statesman was himself well-to-do, upper middle-class, an Oxford classical scholar, with but vague ideas of how the common people lived. He overlooked the fact that the life assurance agent was more than the man who collects the money—he was a living reminder that it was due; he called every week, on pay-day as a rule.

Though, in 1865, the Post Office let it be known that their policies, for sums ranging from twenty to a hundred pounds, gave better returns than the ' private enterprise ' policies, the public remained uninterested. When awkward questions were asked in Parliament about Mr. Gladstone's ' white elephant ' the Government agreed to appoint a select committee to look into the failure of the scheme. Reasons given to this body included:

1. Absence of collectors.

2. Necessity for visits to the Post Office, which was shut when the working man was free and open when he was at work.

3. Too many complicated formalities, including medical examinations when small sums were involved.

The remedy, suggested the committee, was for the Government to enlist additional civil servants to act as agents. But this idea appealed to few people and certainly not to Mr. Gladstone.

However, in a final effort to save the scheme some restrictions were relaxed. Post Office savings could be used for the payment of premiums, and ' medicals ' were waived for sums of less than £25. Administration was transferred from the National Debt Commissioners to the Postmaster General. Yet, in spite of all, Mr. Gladstone's ' white elephant ' grew larger and larger. In the five years following 1884 only 2,810 policies were taken out. The scheme remained moribund, mocking both Mr. Gladstone's logic and his good intentions, until it was finally wound up in 1926.

Of course, some people saw this as further proof of the improvidence of the working class, which had thus spurned the country's efforts to protect it from fraud, and exploitation for profit.

One witness was questioned by parliamentarians on the problem of lapsed policies:

> Can you say upon a general calculation how many policies lapse in the course of a year?
> About two-thirds or three-quarters of them.
> And what is the reason?
> The shiftiness of the working classes.

Yet it was from this ' shifty ' working class that William Booth was enlisting his soldiers.

Chapter Five

COMPETITION

THE Booths, father and son, with their small but quick-to-learn team of assurance pioneers, questioned from the first Westminster's pessimistic and ungenerous assessment of the working class. They saw the miners, factory hands and farm labourers as deserving of compassion, as in need of encouragement to thrift, as sufferers from their own illiteracy, victimized by many who exploited them for gain.

Indeed, The Salvation Army's initial venture into life assurance shows here and there a somewhat naïve faith in the honesty and thriftiness of all workers. This may have been justified of many, even of most, but it still left a large number of the other sort. There were numerous cases of absconding agents, bad debts; there were thousands of lapsed policies. The Army learned its lessons the hard way.

In 1893, as the Army took the plunge from the relative safety of its annuity business, into the deeper waters of life assurance, the Society went further than the law demanded and announced:

> Several societies, it is understood, derive profit from lapses. The Salvation Army proposes to abolish this system of profit-making at the poor man's expense.

It was in 1896, three years later, that the Chief Registrar, official Government watchdog on the life offices, made it obligatory to give notice of arrears and the danger of a lapsed policy. He said:

> The provision is intended to protect members against being thrown out of benefit by the collector not calling upon him. Societies in many cases absolutely maintain themselves by these lapses.

In other ways the new Salvation Army Society showed a competitive spirit:

> Other societies do not grant the privilege of a free policy until after five years' payments have been made. This Society gives a

free paid-up policy provided the assurance shall have been in force two years.

If there is a note of superiority in these early announcements from the infant Society it might be excused on the grounds of outstanding achievement. The early years of any society are the dangerous ones, and there were sceptics who sat back to watch for the inevitable shipwreck of this Salvation Army venture. In fact, the first years, as will be seen, show a rate of growth which made even the rich and long-entrenched life assurance pundits of the City express surprise and admiration.

There were of course doubters, some in the ranks of the Army. With societies falling like leaves in autumn how could this weak growth survive? And what had life assurance to do with saving souls? That was the question.

Chapter Six

RAILTON INTERVENES

ONE great man, the Army's first Commissioner, the scholastic, devout George Scott Railton, saw the Salvation Army Society as another diversionary encroachment by ' commercialism', a word he often used of the ventures into trading, and other business activities, for which Bramwell Booth was mainly responsible and which Railton deplored. Railton was an idealist. Like Francis of Assisi, he loved nothing which might pollute the pure fountain of gospel truth or divert its ministers from complete devotion.

Yet his public protest against Salvation Army assurance, made in the Queen's Hall, London, on Friday, July 6, 1894 (when he appeared barefooted, and in sackcloth and ashes!), is so out of character for the gentle, loyal, always courteous Railton that an explanation is necessary. William Booth was used to Railton's strong convictions and he had allowed him to argue on Salvationist tactics many, many times in the past.

Indeed, Railton had played a key part in laying down lines of Salvationist faith and action. He had lived for eleven years in the Booth home in Gore Road, Hackney, and during that time had endeared himself to the children, becoming a beloved member of the family. He had put all his weight behind the pressure group which persuaded William Booth to assume one-man control of The Christian Mission when the long and frustrating dialogues of the Annual Conference were threatening to wreck the Movement. Compulsory total abstinence for Salvationists and the teaching of holiness as a main plank in the Army's platform were other subjects of the Catherine Booth-George Scott Railton partnership which greatly influenced William Booth.

It must be remembered that when George Scott Railton became the Secretary of The Christian Mission, Bramwell

Booth was but a youth of sixteen, and a sickly one at that. For about ten years Railton was ' chief of staff ' to William Booth, his right-hand man and a decisive influence over many crucial stages in the development of The Salvation Army. So he felt entitled to make his feelings known about any new departure in Salvationist affairs.

What was different in Railton's opposition to Salvation Army life assurance was the startling public intervention, with consequent embarrassment to William Booth, who held Railton in high and affectionate regard. It had always been Railton's method to state his objections and change the Founder's mind if possible but, if not, if the decision went against him, to go on with the war.

A number of factors must be taken into account as a background to Railton's extreme course of action at the Queen's Hall meeting. They deserve consideration, for if Railton, so often right, and always acting out of deepest convictions, was right on this occasion, then justification for the Army's acquisition of an assurance society is lacking.

Railton had been in Germany for four years, and they had been hard years. He had to live in Hamburg, then a Free City, because he had been named as an ' undesirable alien '. He sometimes led gatherings attended by fewer than a dozen people. Meetings were prohibited after 5 p.m. on weekdays and 12 noon on Sundays. Policemen guarded the doors at the halls and collected the tickets which were necessary before admittance could be gained. All in all, the war in Germany was hard and funds were low.

Yet, coming to London to celebrate the Jubilee Celebrations of the Founder's conversion (1844–94) and the twenty-ninth anniversary of the Army, Railton saw a full page of advertisements in *The War Cry* which vaunted a Salvation Army bank, a property company and emigration service, a labour exchange, a portrait studio, a knitting factory, and a travel bureau. There was the match factory which manufactured various sophisticated improvements on the common or garden products, including ladies' ' boudoir ' matches, in splendid enamel boxes.

Side by side with a list of corps which had decreased their order for *The War Cry*, was an appeal for the *Jubilee* 1,000 candidates. And near it another appeal:

SALVATION ARMY LIFE ASSURANCE SOCIETY
Smart energetic men wanted as agents. Salvationists and those who have had industrial assurance experience preferred. Liberal commission—Apply to the Managing Director, 103, Queen Victoria Street, London E.C.4.

To Railton this did not make sense. ' Business ' had never been attractive to him. He had lost a job as shipping clerk because he would not write business letters full of assurances that he knew were not true. Unlike the Founder and Bramwell Booth, who were confident that the Army could take over a business and sanctify it, Railton was afraid that business would take over the Army.

But Railton's opposition to Salvation Army assurance had reasons other than those conjured up by trade, banking and life assurance. He was a mystic, the saint who fills the cloister with prayer and meditation, quite unmindful that the bed and breakfast, the candles and the fire, must be paid for in coins of the realm. Even the most devout of God's children must learn that man—even though he shall not live by bread alone—none the less needs bread if he is to live. Railton and those who took a similar stand with regard to Salvation Army assurance were, without intending to, implying that Bramwell Booth and those others with him in launching the new Society had not fully considered the spiritual pros and cons of what they were doing. But they had.

Major Ernest A. Bremner, the Army's Bank Manager and first Managing Director of Salvation Army assurance put it as follows:

The separation of religion from business is a man-made separation and the very opposite of what God intends.

Bramwell Booth declared where he stood in words which are printed boldly in every issue of *Assurance*:

The pages of this magazine will, I hope, show . . . that this undertaking can be conducted in harmony with the principle laid down by the prophet: ' Her merchandise and her hire shall be holiness unto the Lord.' Holiness unto the Lord—that is our trade mark. Anything that cannot be done in harmony with it must not, shall not, be done by us or ours.

It is now part of the history of The Salvation Army Assurance Society that a galaxy of Army leaders signed a letter of dissent from Railton's public and highly embarrassing action. It said:

My dear General,

With reference to Commissioner Railton's expressions in the public meeting at the Queen's Hall on Friday afternoon last we, whose names appear at the foot of this letter, have thought it necessary to confer together, which we have done today with the following result:

1. We consider such a mode of expressing disagreement with any subject or arrangement which has been endorsed by the General, or any officer acting under his authority, to be utterly wrong and subversive to all discipline. Not only have we no sympathy in such a course, but we do not admit that there are any grounds, or can be any justification, for such remarks as were made.

2. We are quite assured of the rightness and soundness of the principles of the Institutions which he referred to and any reluctance in accepting them can only be because they are not understood.

3. We all feel the importance of your taking some definite action in so grave a matter, but as we cannot but think that Commissioner Railton would never have so acted, but for the physical and mental strain from which he is evidently suffering, we would suggest that you should order the Commissioner upon a lengthened furlough, before coming to any final decision as to the future.

We also think it most important that some reference should be made to Commissioner Railton's statements in the Staff Council being held during this week.

We are, dear General,
        affectionately and faithfully yours,

                    T. Henry Howard
                    John A. Carleton
                    Elijah Cadman
                    Ballington Booth
                    F. de L. Booth-Tucker
                    Thos. B. Coombs
                    Ed. Higgins
                    W. Ridsdel
                    H. Ouchterlony

B—A.U.S.

A postscript read:

Being at Sheffield this morning I was not present at the above council but I most fully endorse what is expressed above as to the wrongness of the action of the Commissioner in that meeting. I have no personal knowledge of the question he referred to but share absolutely and with all my heart the above expressions of entire confidence in the decisions that have been taken by the General and staff in those matters.

A. S. Booth-Clibborn

In fact Railton needed no defenders on physical or mental grounds. William Booth was angry and distressed, but not at all likely to rush into steps to destroy this one voice that cried against him. Railton did have a longish rest, unhappy months, when he was 'out of an appointment' and waiting for the summons from his beloved General. It came; he made his peace and resumed his great work for the Army. William Booth and Railton agreed to differ, though the latter conceded that any further objections of his should not be made in public!

The William Booth–Railton relationship was a special one. No other man could take Railton's place in William Booth's life. The Founder knew that Railton was unworldly in the literal sense of that term. Sometimes William Booth must have wished he could indulge in such luxury—such a mountain-top experience, withdrawn from the plight of the people below, unconcerned about their need and unobliged to organize and finance any world-wide attempt to rescue them.

Chapter Seven

THE FIRST
BOARD MEETING

It soon became clear that this new brain-child of Bramwell Booth, and the small team of assurance experts about him, would produce profits for the Lord's work, not at once, not in vast amounts, but steadily rising. The first year of Salvationist industrial assurance showed the beginning of growth that was startling and soon became so marked that the professional insurance journals commented upon it, while *Assurance*, the house magazine of Salvation Army assurance, could not refrain from boasting that the Army's life assurance growth rate exceeded that of the Prudential—there could be no greater claim than that!

. The secret, of course, was the existence of hundreds of corps, centres of humanity with insurable interests, and legions of dedicated people willing to be enrolled as agents for the new Society. Many of these would have become officers had not some domestic or other circumstance prevented them. The assurance agency was the next best thing, a bread-and-butter living—jam sometimes—with many opportunities to serve God and the Army as premium collections took them down the streets and into the homes of the common people.

In London, if the small headquarters staff lacked knowledge, or made mistakes, there is little evidence of it. Theirs was an assurance office with a difference—both William and Bramwell Booth were at pains to make this clear. In such a mood the fact that they were advancing into fields where mighty life assurance companies were already firmly entrenched mattered little.

As the Army began the Prudential announced that it had issued 10,000,000 policies with a profit on the year's working of £2,000,000, of which sum £1,600,000 had been distributed to policy and shareholders.

The Army saw no need to fear this mammoth or other

mighty life assurance concerns, some of which had a hundred years' start.

There was nothing quite like Salvation Army assurance. True there were other Societies with denominational labels in their title but this was a publicity device only. The Wesleyan and General, of Birmingham, never had official links with the Wesleyans. There is today a Methodist Insurance Company, operating with permission of Conference, but only after giving an undertaking to devote all profits to charities. It has in fact paid over a million pounds into Methodist funds and almost all Methodist Church properties are insured with it. It does not do life assurance business.

The first board meeting of the Methodist and General after the Army's acquisition of it took place on June 4, 1891. The Acting Secretary, James Field, was the man in charge of the transition. Years later Commissioner Samuel Hurren was to cast his mind back to his youthful days spent in the service of The Salvation Army Assurance Society. He wrote in *Assurance*: ' Sergeant-Major Field, of " The Royal " and Clapton Congress Hall, looked in at head office occasionally for a chat and the giving of advice and, in this as in other ways, proved himself a good man and a true Salvationist.'

At the beginning Field produced twenty-eight nominations duly completed by guarantors of the old Methodist and General. He also put on the table the copy of a resolution:

> Resolved that the Charter of Incorporation, the Director's Roll Book, and half a dozen copies of the Deed of Settlement be handed over to The Salvation Army.

In addition to Field the board was composed of:

> William Booth, General.
> Bramwell Booth, Chief of Staff.
> Geo. Lampard, Grocer.
> E. A. Bremner, Salvation Army officer.
> Thomas Cooksey, Hatter.
> Edward Higgins, Salvation Army officer.
> E. J. Townsend, Salvation Army officer.
> Wilfred L. Simpson, Salvation Army officer

On June 30th, Secretary Field handed over the precious Charter—worth £20,000—to The Salvation Army. At this particular time press and public were watching to see if William Booth's deeds would match his grand words in *In Darkest England and the Way Out*. Following its publication in 1890, in newspapers and public utterances, Professor Thomas Huxley and others had charged the Founder with financial maladministration, and he was chronically short of money.

After taking over the Charter Bramwell Booth wrote to the Founder:

I have to report progress in the organization of the Assurance Society. You will remember that you approved our plan up to the point of taking over the Charter of the 'Methodist and General'. The general idea was, while keeping the Society legally alive, to elect new guarantee members, who should then elect new directors, that the change of name would immediately follow and we could proceed in due course with annuity and other business.

Before taking over the Charter we, acting on the advice of Sargant,* arranged so that all the liabilities of the old Company were discharged, with the result that though having a legal it had no business existence. . . . We have already done some business and have in hand inquiries for further annuities representing probably six or seven thousand pounds of purchase money.

The security of the annuitants is of course their chief concern. No one comes to us, or will come to this Society, except for their faith in, and desire to help, The Salvation Army.

*Afterwards Lord Justice Sargant.

Chapter
Eight

NEW SOCIETY
—OLD NAME

AT the board meeting on June 30, 1891, at 119 Salisbury Square, it was proposed ' that the name of the Society be changed to " The Salvation Army Insurance Society " '. It was so resolved. No one seemed to notice the excessive optimism of this proposal or its faulty terminology. The Board of Trade might shut an eye toward a transfer, as between one religious group and another, but it would not allow the wide publicity that legal recognition would give before the new possessors of the charter had demonstrated their financial acumen and their organizing ability. Besides, the Board of Trade did not really approve of such transfers. The Army had to wait a long time before permission was given.

The phrase, ' Insurance Society ', might hold good for the United States, but in Britain and most other countries a policy that depends on a certainty, either the death of the person named on the policy or the arrival at an age stipulated under a policy, is life assurance. Protection against contingencies such as fire, flood, theft, accident are generally termed insurance. One could say that assurance must happen: insurance may happen.

It was plain in these first days how much the Army depended on ' the laity '. A Mr. E. Widdowson took the chair at the June 30th meeting. Field was still Secretary. Both men were old Methodist and General directors. Knox, Burbridge and Cropper were invited to undertake the audit of what was in effect a new Society, whatever its old name might be. They were asked to do this free of charge, or at a nominal fee, ' having regard to the benevolent nature and limited scope of the Society's operations '.

But ' limited scope ' also proved to be an inaccurate term. Indeed, all the records show that this new baby proved to be an embarrassingly precocious child, with a rate of growth not only a cause of astonishment to its own managers but also to the life assurance world at large. However, the auditors accepted a mere ten guineas for their first year's work for the Society.

An account was opened at the City Bank in the name of four directors. New Articles of Association were proposed and accepted. Annuities continued to come in mainly from the better-off friends of the Army who were quite willing to let William Booth have their capital in return for his pledge to let them have a living year by year until they no longer had a life to live. Miss Gribble was one of the first. Aged forty-two, she let the Army have her £1,000 for an annuity of sixty-five pounds per annum. So many annuities came in that the board had to consider an investment policy. This must have been a greatly appreciated luxury for Bramwell Booth. Hitherto his task had been to keep debts down to manageable proportions.

On August 21, 1891, at an extraordinary general meeting at 101 Queen Victoria Street, William Booth was appointed ' Patron of the Society '; Ernest A. Bremner its Managing Director and James Field its Secretary. If the beginners in life assurance, for as such we can describe Bramwell Booth, John Carleton, Edward Higgins, T. Henry Howard and Bremner, felt uncertain, they did not show it. They opened their board meetings in prayer and faced the banks, the City, the financial press and the big life offices unafraid. A Mr. Cockburn, an actuary, had been asked for life tables and the scent of progress was in the nostrils of the men around the board room table. The working classes were waking up to their need for life assurance. The Salvation Army was ready to do its share in providing them with what they wanted.

Chapter
Nine

CARLETON'S 'CANARY'

THE first Commissioner Managing Director, John A. Carleton, deserves a special niche in this history of the Society. No man had charge of it for so lengthy a period, twenty-five years, from 1894 to 1919, and an additional year 1925–26, as Joint Managing Director with Colonel William Maxwell. He remained Chairman of the Board of Directors until his passing in 1934—a period of forty years in office.

Carleton was ' a character '—as were so many of the Army's early-day leaders. He was fond of salmon fishing and cycling, the latter hobby being maintained long after he attained the rank of Commissioner—the mind boggles at the thought of a present-day Commissioner riding a bicycle!

His high value to the Army, from the time he became an officer in 1881, lay in the fact that he was a competent business man; these were in very short supply. He came from a middle-class background, in Northern Ireland, having been converted in the 1859 revival. He met the Army at Londonderry and at first did not approve of the women preachers whom William Booth had appointed to lead the invasion. But Carleton soon saw the light, and asked the Army to open a corps at Ligoniel, where he lived with a young wife in what the local folk called ' the Big House '.

He was an executive in one of Sir William Ewart's mills and, for some time, was reluctant to throw in his lot with the Salvationists, who were regarded with mixed feelings by the local inhabitants. But presently Carleton took the plunge—at the Penitent-form. Soon afterwards his home was being used by William Booth for an officers' meeting, and as a billet for those who must remain overnight.

On his return to London William Booth, in response to

Carleton's pleadings, sent an officer to open a corps at Ligoniel and in the first month 150 seekers were recorded. The kitchen in ' the Big House ' was used twice a week for meetings. It seated seventy people. Carleton and his wife found themselves more and more involved with this Salvation Army and its war. Before many months had passed the furniture in ' the Big House ' was auctioned and the Carletons left for London where, for the next two years, the gentle, highly capable Ulsterman became Private Secretary to Bramwell Booth. In 1883 he was appointed head of the Army's Trade Department, then housed in a basement of 101 Queen Victoria Street. He held the post for ten years, during which time he saw ' Trade ' grow until it employed 350 people and outgrow its basement to take over new premises in Clerkenwell Road.

At the same time he was publisher and printer of *The War Cry* and the rest of the string of Army papers and books. Perhaps more to the point, as proof of his worth, is the fact that he was a euphonium player at his beloved home corps Penge—having learned to play at the age of forty because there was a vacancy which no other seemed ready to fill. He made a mark on the corps which survives to this day. Penge will always be Carleton's corps. He loved it so much, was so ardent and energetic in its activities, that there were lamentations in other quarters that he could not be persuaded to go ' specialing '. One of his achievements, was to commence at Penge the Army's first officially recognized songster brigade.

Another claim to fame is that he was seized with an inspired idea, which he wrote down and passed on to William Booth as he was leading a meeting at the Exeter Hall, London. The year was 1886, and the Founder was gravely concerned about the Army's inability, because of lack of funds, to meet the demands made upon it. The note had a Franciscan touch about it:

> By going without my pudding every day for a year I calculate I shall save fifty shillings. This will I do and will remit the amount named as quickly as possible.

The note was written on one of the yellow forms which
had been distributed to the congregation to be filled in with
pledges of financial support. They were humorously
referred to as ' canaries '. The Founder held Carleton's
' canary ' up for all to see. He said:

> I do not think that any of my officers ought to go without
> their pudding for a whole year. They need all the food they can
> get, and probably more.

Soon afterwards a letter was received at International
Headquarters which read:

> I was at your meeting at the Exeter Hall and agree with you
> that your officers should not be asked to do without their pudding
> for a year. In order that the officer who filled in that interesting
> ' canary ' may not have to do this I enclose a cheque for fifty
> shillings. Please let him have his pudding.

One of William Booth's strongest qualities was his
ability to grasp quickly at other people's good suggestions
and use them to great effect. He said to Bramwell Booth
and Carleton:

> There's an idea here. While it is true that we ought not to ask
> officers to do without anything for a whole year, I see no reason
> why we should not ask them to go without something every day
> for a week, and to give the proceeds to help the work we have
> on hand (**Puddings and Policies** by Sidney Williams).

In the autumn of that year the first Self-Denial Effort
was launched and the sum of nearly £5,000 raised.

Carleton took charge of The Salvation Army Assurance
Society in the year that it branched out into industrial
assurance. Before then its annuity business and its mortgages on properties made it a suitable charge for Bremner
and the Property Department. Now the Society was to
become self-contained and stand on its own feet. Instead
of being sustained by The Salvation Army it would now
play a great part in supporting the Army. As we have seen,
it would be some years before this aim was reached, but
meanwhile Carleton was the chief architect as the Society
was built up in funds, manpower, efficiency and its over-all
purpose—to conduct a life assurance society to the glory of
God and the salvation of souls.

Chapter
Ten
THE SICK
AND WOUNDED

LARGE in the story of The Salvation Army Assurance Society is Commissioner Samuel Hurren, who joined it when it was still the Methodist and General. He went to it reluctantly, being of the opinion that his former positions of private secretary to 'Grandpa' Higgins, and later to Commissioner and Consul Booth-Tucker, were much to be preferred to 'helping Carleton', which was the formula for his work as described by Bramwell Booth, who made the appointment.

Hurren found it to be a somewhat illusory description. For many months he did not even see Carleton, but was 'pushed around', as he describes it, having to help just anybody. When at last he was indeed the great man's secretary—and secretary to the Bank and the Head Office Council—there was one flaw in his qualifications. Those who can yet remember the torrents of eloquence that could flow from the lips of Samuel Hurren, will sympathize with him and admire the honesty with which he confessed his dilemma: 'I never could enjoy listening to discussions and not taking part in them.'

Hurren was aware of George Scott Railton's views on life assurance and his public protest against the launching of a Salvation Army Assurance Society. But though a ready writer in *Assurance* he picks his way delicately around the incident. He wrote:

> Many felt as I felt in the early days about life assurance work, and did not take to the new departure with any degree of affection. Indeed, the whole idea of assurance business took a great deal of putting over, especially among officers, not a few of whom had sold up everything—including assurance policies, watches and almost every other accessory—before coming into the work; though some, it is true, had later weakly compromised by wearing a 5s. 'Waterbury' [watch] attached to a piece of string or bootlace. I myself was some time in the 'Life' before I took a policy, and possessed no watch until late middle age.

The Commissioner goes on to record, writing from

retirement down on the south-east coast, that the Assurance Society staff were a mixed bag. One was found to be running a 'get-rich-quick' business not far from Head Office, supposedly in his spare time. But it was in the Society's time, and when he was discovered his connection with Salvation Army assurance was soon ended.

There were other occasional black sheep, Hurren relates, such as the agent who sent in proposals on dead men, their names copied from tombstones, declaring that 'they were in good health at present', and collecting the fees before the policies lapsed in a few weeks. He then found himself unable to meet the charges back, and great was the fall thereof. Another black sheep took ordinary branch premiums, giving unofficial receipts, and flourished like a green bay tree until the assured died. Then it was found that the deceased's policy had been lapsed for some time although his premiums were up to date. But such rare incidents happen in all societies.

Samuel Hurren, known as the 'boy Captain', found that his education proceeded apace at Head Office. He once witnessed 'a scrap on the stairs of " 107 "', between two Superintendents, both of whom soon left us'.

Chief Inspector Alfred Braine and young Hurren were fellow soldiers and songsters at Penge Corps, where the redoubtable Carleton was the Songster Leader. As related earlier Carleton was fond of cycling, regarding it, as he did most things, with the utmost seriousness. Braine and Hurren sometimes found that the Managing Director's zeal was too much of a good thing. 'Alfred Braine always knew when the moment had come to let the " guv'nor " enjoy his triumph alone.' Then the two turned off at a side lane and took a short cut home.

In William Booth's mind, and in many others, an argument for The Salvation Army Assurance Society was the fact that it could be, in part, a haven for sick and wounded officers, casualties of the salvation war. The Founder made no apologies for this function, mentioning it openly when explaining his hopes for the Society.

It was a function well-fulfilled, though not so much in these days as in the past and never so extensively as suggested by the agent who, according to Hurren, informed a prospective client that he should take out a Salvation Army policy if only on compassionate grounds: ' You should see 'em at Head Office, rows upon rows of 'em: consumptions, hearts, hystericals and what-not.'

But, seriously, time gave ample proof of the great value of the role, envisaged by William Booth, for this practical and compassionate aspect of Salvation Army assurance. Not that the men and women remained sick or failed to make good as assurance officers. There are many instances where men relieved of corps work on genuine health grounds, and put to life assurance work, both in London and the provinces, have shown themselves highly adaptable, learning their new duties quickly and efficiently. Doubtless, Commissioner Hurren, when he became British Commissioner, modified his views about sick officers. He certainly had cause to value the Society's role as a haven for a proportion of health cases among his corps officers.

Though Hurren was not enthusiastic about being appointed to Salvation Army life assurance he was distinctly sorry to leave it. By this time, as Carleton's secretary, he was responsible for allowing or disallowing claims. At first, because this task involved extensive study of real or alleged maladies, he had to consult *Quain's Medical Dictionary*, and one day, while poring over the details of a gruesome disease, Samuel Hurren ' passed out ', full length on the office floor, becoming conscious again to find Commissioner Carleton and Alfred Braine applying first aid.

Of course there were occasions when claims had to be rejected and Hurren did not flinch from the decision—he came early to the realization that ' the acceptance of responsibility is the road to advancement '. Sometimes, when a legal action was threatened, after Samuel Hurren had rejected a claim, the Managing Director would have to take the final decision. Usually the threatened action was abandoned, proof of Hurren's good judgment.

Chapter Eleven

LIFE ASSURANCE
FOR CHILDREN

THE year 1897 marked the end of an experiment which had proved to be an embarrassment to the Society, its agents in particular. It concerned ' infantile assurance ', as the Army's magazine *Assurance* often termed it. In the hungry forties of William Booth's youth, Britain was in the throes of a terrible economic depression. It was the decade of Ireland's potato famine and of high-priced bread, caused by the iniquitous Corn Laws, repealed in 1846. In that year, also, any assurance on a child under six years was forbidden by Act of Parliament. Infants died readily; their ailments were numerous and their remedies inadequate. Queen Anne had lost all her fourteen children. Much later, 1861, Prince Albert, in the haven of Windsor Castle, died of typhoid brought on, it was stated, by contaminated water and bad drains. If death, from such causes, could strike in the royal palaces, how much stronger were its terrors in the poorer districts of the great towns and cities?

Charles Kingsley had written to his wife in 1849, the year William Booth came to live in London:

> I was yesterday in the cholera district of Bermondsey; and, oh God! what I saw! People having no water to drink—hundreds of them—but the water of the common sewer which stagnates full of . . . dead fish, cats and dogs under their very windows.

Ten years later London experienced ' The Great Stink ' when a hot summer and low rainfall caused the Thames to stagnate. As the river was to all intents and purposes a sewer, people who had to cross Westminster Bridge held a handkerchief over nose and mouth. Unfortunate Members of Parliament deliberated behind curtains soaked in chloride of lime. William Booth was at Gateshead at this time but he knew his London. The Thames remained a sewer until the Metropolitan Water Board came into being in 1903.

No wonder that children died! While William Booth

walked the streets of London and raised his voice in Methodist chapels

> the overcrowded cemeteries within the City walls had become raised far above street level, and ' in the 218 acres of London's burial grounds, 20,000 adults and nearly 30,000 youths and children were interred each year ', so that the grave-diggers had to exercise great ingenuity in inserting new corpses into old graves, and resorted to dreadful expedients in making room for future burials.*

Whenever Parliament discussed life assurance, which was frequently, the bogey of child assurance would be raised, although there was little evidence that it was the murderous system that many people alleged it to be. Today, in the light of history, no proof exists that widespread baby-killing was fostered by the availability of child life assurance. There were a number of child murders, some deaths from neglect and starvation, but no general link with assurance claims has ever been established. What did exist was hunger, disease, exposure, and shocking conditions of child labour only slowly alleviated by the efforts of Shaftesbury and his helpers. In 1850, after evidence that some parents did misappropriate life assurance payments on the death of a child, Parliament limited the sum payable on ' infantile assurance ' to the actual cost of the funeral, which must not exceed £3.

In 1890 the House of Lords returned to the subject with a motion that life assurance payments on children should be made direct to the undertaker. There was some evidence that, in a number of cases, the money was not being devoted to the payment of funeral expenses. Undertakers who were not paid often had no redress. The parents of a dead child were, in some instances, destitute. So yet another Parliamentary Select Committee was appointed. Before this, Will Crooks, who later became famous as a Labour leader, protested strongly against the insinuations behind the Committee's terms of reference, and the threat to deprive parents of the right to do as they would with their own. He was scornful of suggestions that small

* *Edwin Chadwick*, Lewis.

sums, always insufficient, could create temptations powerful enough to turn working-class parents into ghouls. On the contrary, Crooks said, child life assurance enabled parents to practise thrift in order to keep up payment on policies, and enabled them to do without charity or recourse to pawnshops—thereby strengthening their self-respect. Moreover, a result of prohibition of the sort intended would call for a return to the old ' whip-round ' in the pub. That was a worse solution.

Crooks added that he did not see why 999 sheep should be punished for the sins of one black sheep, and eventually the Lord's Committee recommended that the proposal to pay money to the undertaker direct was against the public interest.

Shortly after this, in 1894, the Army's Society decided to act contrary to the Select Committee's recommendation, giving prominence in its prospectus to the following announcement:

> In order to protect the interest of children the Society reserves to itself the right to pay the funeral and medical expenses direct to the undertaker and doctor, instead of handing the sum assured to the parents in such cases as, in the opinion of the Society, were open to suspicion.*

The Society had earlier announced, in its first prospectus (1893), that it had determined not to transact infantile assurance business in the ordinary sense.

> At the same time a scheme is in contemplation whereby all the benefits of an assurance are secured without, it is thought, attendant objection. Arrangements are in progress by which the Society will provide for the whole cost of the funeral, together with a sum to cover incidental expenses such as doctor's bills, etc.

But, in 1896, with the redoubtable Commissioner John A. Carleton as Managing Director, and Vice-Chairman to Bramwell Booth, this paternal attitude on the part of the Society was modified. There had been considerable criticism from rival life assurance companies and also from Salvation Army assurance agents who found the rule disadvantageous.

* *The Story of The Salvation Army Assurance Society Ltd.*, Rivers (1935).

Some parents, finding unusual conditions attached to child coverage, resented the implication and took their business elsewhere.

Carleton's modification, in the 1896 prospectus, was as follows:

> If a child shall die before attaining the age of 5 years, the Society reserves to itself the right to only pay the sum assured upon the production of satisfactory evidence that the amount has been, or will be, expended upon the funeral and medical expenses of the assured, and such other expenses as the Society shall consider to have been necessary in connection with the illness and death of the assured. While reserving to itself this right, the Society, under ordinary circumstances, will pay the sum assured without enforcing the foregoing condition. The right will only be exercised in exceptional cases, where there are reasons to believe that the life was assured for wrong purposes.

Sir Edward Clarke and other prominent men commended the Army's stand but time showed that the Salvation Army directors had been ill-advised in this special proviso also. Agents found the clause embarrassing and competitors made the most of the Army's disadvantage. In an article in *Assurance* Brigadier David Cuthbert reported that in parts of the country he had visited agents

> of certain societies, jealous of our progress and prosperity (in spite of the clause!) actually follow our agents on their rounds. Where they leave policies their way-layers call at the house after they have gone, and ask to see the policies and if they find one on a child among them they attack the inoffensive clause.

However, the clause proved to be indefensible, and sprung from Carleton's ultra-cautious disposition. Will Crooks had read the public mind more accurately when he defended working-class parents against the innuendo.

Carleton withdrew the rule, announcing as follows:

SPECIAL CLAUSES IN INFANTILE POLICIES

> It will be within the recollection of many of our readers that, from time to time, very serious statements have been made in the press and elsewhere as to the evils resulting from infantile assurance, and it has been freely stated that children, especially young children, are systematically neglected and abused to hasten their death, in order that the parents might obtain the amount for which their lives were assured.
>
> The Directors, at the time of the preparation of the infantile

policies of this Society, had this matter very prominently before them; and, although they were of opinion that, if this evil did exist, it was infinitesimally small, they carefully considered whether the children could not in some way be safe-guarded. With this purpose in view, the following clause was made one of the conditions of all infantile policies issued by the Society:

' If the assured shall die before attaining the age of five years, the Society shall not be bound to pay the sum assured, or any part thereof, except upon the production of satisfactory evidence that the amount has been expended upon the funeral and medical expenses of the assured and such other expenses as the Society shall consider to have been necessary in connection with the illness and death of the assured.'

Thousands of such policies have been issued, and many claims paid, but in only one instance has it been necessary to use the power given by this clause, and even in that case the explanations given were satisfactory.

Under these circumstances, the Directors have decided to cancel the clause, both as regards existing policies as well as those issued from this date.

The Assurance Agents' Review gave the funeral oration for the clause:

After four years The Salvation Army puts on record that only in one solitary case was there ever enough suspicion to warrant them putting their special precautionary clause into operation. The insurance world is under a very substantial debt to The Salvation Army for carrying out such a brave and useful experiment.

Chapter Twelve

THE AGENT

' LIFE assurance seems to be a business that you must go and get,' said a witness before the inquiry into the failure of Mr. Gladstone's National Post Office Life Assurance Scheme. ' The foundation of the industrial assurance system is the agent,' said Lord Parmoor.

He was referring, of course, to the new kind of life assurance that catered for the working classes. The Old Amicable Society, which began in 1706, and others after it, could demand that relatively prosperous prospective clients, certainly not of the working class, should appear in person before the board. It was usually banker's draft payment and what is now called ordinary branch assurance. Before 1852 the Prudential, now a world giant among assurance companies, was a modest affair, having struggled on for years at a slow rate as a mutual assurance, investment and loan association. But in that year a group of workmen asked if the company would consider ' small assurance, of £20 and upwards, payable by weekly instalments '. This was, without anyone perceiving it, a great moment in life assurance history.

Of course, the friendly societies already existing were, in great part, collecting societies, but they were a far different proposition. They gave sickness benefits and burial grants, not scientific calculation of life expectancy, life tables, profits for policy-holders from investment gains. Industrial life assurance was to be provision for ' the common people ' of a kind already established for the well-to-do.

The ' Pru '* admits that the request from the group of working men was not received with any great enthusiasm. The Board asked for tables and were told by the experts that a scheme was feasible, yet two years went by before

---

*A Century of Service, compiled by R. W. Barnard, for the Prudential, and *A History of Industrial Life Assurance*, by Dermot Morrah, George Allen and Unwin (1955).

action was taken. Even then the venture into ' poor man's assurance ' was so little understood that the ' Pru ' directors, when considering the centres where their agencies should be established, first turned their thoughts to Brighton and other ' respectable ' areas rather than the Midlands, London, Yorkshire and Lancashire, where existed the teeming working class called into being by the Industrial Revolution.

But wise counsels prevailed. Branch offices were opened where the working people lived and ' the man from the Prudential ' began that doorstep canvassing that made him that widely recognized and beneficent figure presented by the advertisements. Yet it was a slow start and more than once the ' Pru's ' new venture seemed likely to founder. After the first check on progress it was found that the total premium income, from all sources, was only £4,000, while the cost of branch offices and the appointment of superintendents ran to £35,000.

As has been stated, The Salvation Army Assurance Society's rate of growth exceeded this. However, the unfavourable comparison would not hold good for long. Total Prudential ordinary branch and industrial branch premium income for 1966 was £187,000,000, the industrial branch alone being nearly one and a half million a week. In its first decade the ' Pru's ' progress gave no hint of such stupendous success and *Assurance* printed the comparisons by which the ' Pru ' was shown to have had a slower growth than the Salvation Army assurance. This comparison was to some extent loaded for, in 1855, the Prudential had only one year's full industrial branch growth—and this was at the pioneer period. All who came after benefited by what had gone before and, as will be seen, the Army was last in the field among the companies named.

This is not to deny that the Salvation Army growth rate was remarkably good. It was, and the main reason was the existing chain of corps, and the availability and type of agent who could be enlisted from those corps. In most cases, when applied to industrial life assurance, the blend of Christian idealism, social purpose and plain hard-working agency collecting was irresistible and gave the Army its excellent start.

The first 'Agents' Instructions ' were issued by Major Ernest A. Bremner in 1894. In 1896 Carleton revised them and had this to say:

> Every new departure of The Salvation Army has had the curious eyes of thousands of critics fixed upon it, and it is not at all likely that its life assurance business will be treated differently.
>
> It is essential, therefore, that the agents of this Society should be exceptionally *good* men. Not only good *business* men, who will put forth every effort and use every bit of talent God has given them, to make their agency a success, but *godly* men, who in all their business affairs will guard against doing anything inconsistent with those principles which have made The Salvation Army into such a powerful religious organization—the wonder of the world.
>
> In carrying on his work, the Salvation Army assurance agent has many opportunities of doing spiritual work. He has access to hundreds of families, week by week, with whom he soon becomes on friendly terms; and there is little doubt that with tact and wisdom he can not only prevail upon them to provide against the death of the body, but can also in many cases direct their attention to the importance of securing the eternal welfare of the soul.
>
> The Salvation Army assurance agent has, in fact, as many opportunities of doing good as a Salvation Army officer, and it is confidently anticipated by the Directors that this Society will become a valuable adjunct of The Salvation Army, and that through the efforts of the agents many soldiers should be added to its ranks.

The agent was advised to

> approach the corps Captain in a proper spirit with a view to holding a meeting in the Salvation Army barracks and bringing before the soldiers and friends the advantages and benefits of the Society. . . . The agent must be careful, no matter what provocation he may receive, not to say anything reflecting on any other society or company.
>
> Proposals from persons of intemperate habits, or from persons directly engaged in the drink traffic, will not be entertained under any circumstances.

There is an odd proviso relating to proposals for sums of £25 or over: the social position of proposers must be taken into account.

> The Superintendent or Assistant Superintendent must furnish a certificate of the health and social position of the person pro-

posing. . . . In cases of proposals from persons in humble circumstances, or of advanced age, limited amounts only can be accepted.

The Victorian nonconformist conscience, rather than
actuarial realities, seems to be the basis for the next regu-
lation:

> Proposals may be taken upon children when fourteen days
> old, but proposals upon the lives of illegitimate children under
> three years of age must not be taken excepting by the special
> permission of the Head Office.

In an early issue of *Assurance* Adjutant John Rivers
wrote of the Army assurance agent's qualifications:

> People generally do not care for an agent to call upon them
> who is surly as a bear and some agents do not appear to realize
> this. He must be cheerful . . . he should notice the baby and so
> win the mother's heart.
> What mother does not think her baby the finest that ever was
> born—and there is no reason why any act of yours should dis-
> illusion her. . . . A bag of sweets is a very good thing to carry
> with you; one to the baby will make him good friends with you.

Adjutant Rivers does not explain how the agent is to pay
for the sweets, for presumably, Chief Office would not
allow them as expenses. He went on:

> Don't groan about your earnings; that is your fault.
> Don't make them believe you are next door to the workhouse.
> Don't talk about your troubles; they have enough of their own.

In July, 1898, the Chief Inspector wrote:

> Do not shuffle up to the door like a beggar, and ask for
> premiums as though you were asking a favour; and, when arrears
> have accumulated, go strong for the payment of the total amount
> owing. Make those in arrears feel that they *owe* the amount, and
> that it is a debt due to the Society. Always have the *amount owing
> up to date* ready in your mind before knocking at the door; and
> when your knock is answered, say, ' Let me see, this makes five
> weeks due, Mrs. ———; that will be 2s. 6d.' Say it respectfully,
> and do not be content with one week's payment if more can be
> reasonably obtained.

Chapter Thirteen

FRUITS OF SUCCESS

IN 1898 the Society was asked to send a suitable officer to lecture to the cadets. The Head Office Manager was chosen. He gave passing mention to life assurance in general but concentrated on the Army's 'Apostles of Assurance'. It was gratifying to the lecturer, at this early date, to find that half the cadets were policy-holders with the Salvation Army Society.

Other indications of the acceptance of the Society was a general chorus of commendation from the insurance and financial Press. Praise there had been before but now attacks were rare and eulogy so frequent that it must have created the danger of complacency. *The Assurance Agents' Review* reported as follows:

> The Salvation Army Assurance Society is beyond assault on the matter of finance. It is as stable and sound as the Bank of England. . . .
> The Salvation Army, a new office which had its way to make in the face of the opposition of a host of powerful competitors . . . has . . . been made the target of interested attacks. . . . The Prudential has had to submit to this process. The Refuge has had it. The British Workman's (later known as the Britannic) has had it, and every other office that stands for anything today. Therefore it is not surprising The Salvation Army has the same ordeal to go through.

Other papers joined in the chorus of praise. But one, *The Assurance Agents' Chronicle*, offered a precise reason for the unique success of the Society, almost certainly the correct one. In referring to a premium income increase of £11,000 the paper went on:

> These achievements are very striking and remarkable although when one considers the inestimable advantage which the very complete and all-pervasive organization of the Army afforded for the adoption and application of the system of industrial life assurance, they are not so much to be wondered at.

In this way were the proud men at the helm of the Society reminded that their extraordinary success was due to the Army at large—the corps, the soldiery, the goodwill, and the type of agent enlisted from the corps.

'In the matter of development of connection The Salvation Army is out of sight of any other office,' commented one paper. Indeed, the figures were eloquent:

Office	No. of Years	Date of Account	Prem. Income
Salvation Army	5	1898	£59,250
General Friendly	5	1889	£2,260
British Workman (now Britannic)	6	1872	£4,698
Refuge	6	1870	£9,120
Prudential	7	1855	£3,500
Pearl	7	1872	£9,343
British Legal	9	1872	£7,342
London and Manchester	13	1882	£15,732

In 1898 came the decision to start 'a monthly journal, under the editorship of a Mr. Clutterbuck, who shall receive 35/– per week with other work placed upon him'. This was that same Clutterbuck who a year earlier had perpetrated that enormous *faux pas* of reporting, in *The Young Soldier*, a Crystal Palace review by the Founder that did not take place (see page 47).

The Society was forced to take a more realistic attitude toward people employed in the drink trade. There had been complaints, from Burton-on-Trent, of a clause totally prohibiting the assurance of persons employed in the breweries. The newly adjusted clause read:

> The assured shall not be employed in a distillery, or brewery, hotel, or public house, or other place used for the manufacture of beer, wines or spirits, unless so stated in the policy.

Expansion was now so rapid that it is possible to detect signs of undue haste in selecting staff, and other errors of judgment caused by pressure of progress. A three months' 'stocktaking' of agents revealed that while new agents numbered 155, resignations or dismissals numbered 154. A Superintendent absconded with £31 of the Society's money, and the minutes record sadly that 'all efforts to trace him have failed'.

There was a shock when the first six months' accounts of *Assurance* were examined. It had been laid down that the paper must pay its way and, with a sale of about 4,000, at 2d., it was confidently believed that it would do so. But revenue was £267 15s. 4d., against costs of £414 0s. 11d.

Commissioner Carleton cared not for this and it was decided to ask for estimates from ' outside ', that is, from non-Salvationist printers. This was a brave thing to do and one imagines that Bramwell Booth wot not of it. But such healthy competition caused the Army printer to reduce his estimate considerably and he retained the contract.

Meanwhile, if any believed that any preferential treatment from the Society went with salvation soldiership, or officer's rank, they soon discovered their error. The Salvation Army Society might have plus-elements in it but it was none the less a business, conducted on scientific lines. The calculations of the actuary embraced both the just and the unjust, the convert and the Commissioner. Carleton's impartial eye saw to it that the tables were equally applied. Commissioner Edward Higgins, ' now on the high seas ' as the minutes record, journeying to missionary service in India, shall pay ' £1 10s. extra on his premiums during such time as he is in India '. With cholera, dysentery, and other killing diseases endemic abroad, there was a price to pay for missionary service just as there was, in Kipling's words, a price of Empire.

Yet, amid all this swift adventure, the wheels of business creaked sometimes a little, as when Commissioners Carleton, Thomas Coombs and James Hay, with Colonels Smith and Arthur Bates, deliberated solemnly, and at some length, whether they could accept the services of another office boy. Eventually they reached a decision that ' one named Roberts shall be engaged at 7s. per week '.

Commissioner Coombs, zealous in his new seat on the board, moved that ' no increase in salary or other mark of approval shall be given to any employee of the Society within six months of his being reprimanded for any cause '. This Draconian rule, rather astonishingly, won the approval of the Board, which had Bramwell Booth in the chair. But someone seems to have had second thoughts and sought legal advice. The Army's solicitor gave it as his opinion that 'the resolution could not be operative', and it was rescinded.

Chapter Fourteen

'ASSURANCE'

THE official journal of The Salvation Army Assurance Society was founded in May, 1898. The first editor was ' Brother Geo. Clutterbuck ', already mentioned on page 44 of this story. He had been the editor of *The Young Soldier* but suffered grievous ill health, and had also been the victim of a most unfortunate mishap when, as editor, he had caused *The Young Soldier* to carry a report of a great March Past at the Crystal Palace in the arena known as the Oval. The paper went to press before the event but, as the Founder was to review the parade, and as it concerned young people, editor Clutterbuck inserted a report and an artist's impression of the great occasion.

But a terrific thunderstorm made the Oval into a lake, washed out the parade and put finish to Staff-Captain Clutterbuck's term as *The Young Soldier* editor.

But it was a fortunate event for the newly launched Salvation Army Assurance Society magazine. Clutterbuck gave rein to a team of gifted writers: Hurren, Latham, Braine, Cuthbert, Rivers, Nicholson and others. The magazine was lively, humorous, helpful—a skilfully amalgam of life assurance and Salvationist material. It played an important part not only in the formative years of the Society but in its continuing progress. The first issues reflected the spirit of the times, and one of the most simple errors would be to read those early numbers with the amused hindsight that is often generated by twentieth-century ' superiority '. From the first, *Assurance* set a high standard of writing, variety and enterprise, passing on necessary information, correcting error, bolstering *morale*, lending cohesion to a new, widely scattered organization.

It seems to have had a free hand in areas where today a stricter supervision would be exercised. This is usually a reward of pioneers and can be noticed in the early years of other Salvation Army papers. What is one to make of the following notice, for example, which so flagrantly conflicts with the social methods of The Salvation Army and also with William Booth's ideal life assurance agent?

> Slum business is no good to either agents or a society, and an agent who desires success and promotion will keep out of the slums. Good business from respectable neighbourhoods is more difficult to obtain, but once secured it is almost certain to pay well. In fact, one policy from a good neighbourhood is ultimately worth more than a dozen in the slums.*

This is probably excellent commercial life assurance policy but it is not a good line of reasoning for the Salvationist. Yet these conflicts of interests were inevitable. As will be seen, the hostility of other life assurance companies, and the strength of professional competition, helped to create a tension between Salvation Army life assurance business on the one hand and Bramwell Booth's declaration of ' holiness unto the Lord ' on the other. This created confusion among the early policy-makers and writers in *Assurance*.

Consider the ambivalence in the report reprinted in *Assurance*, on ' Old-Age Pensions in Australia ':

> The working of the old-age pensions scheme in Victoria is a memorable example of mistaken calculations. Sir George Turner calculated that there would be 6,000 applicants for pensions, and he ear-marked £75,000 to provide for the first half of 1901. But already nearly eleven thousand pensions have been granted, and the number still grows.
>
> Sir George Turner's figures, in a word, will be more than doubled; and Victoria must either provide over £300,000 a year for old-age pensions or break faith with its aged clients and cheat the expectations it has kindled. Mr. Peacock declares that Victoria cannot provide so great a sum for this purpose, and he has asked the various benevolent societies throughout the State to assist the authorities in protecting the public revenue from undeserving applicants. The old-age pensions scheme, thus crudely undertaken, has had some curious results.
>
> It has half-emptied at least some of the benevolent asylums. Some of the pensioned have celebrated their newly found independence by getting gloriously drunk and making their appearance in the police courts. Some old people who were really well-to-do have secured pensions by false statements, and are to be prosecuted for perjury. Amongst the pensioned are

Assurance, July, 1898.

some justices of the peace, who have been called upon to resign their commissions. Sir George Turner's old-age scheme, in brief. is an evil political legacy to his successor.

Of course the life offices of those days looked with apprehension on state intervention in insurance affairs, Mr. Gladstone's efforts, and Bismarck's in Germany, having attracted world-wide attention and some emulation. The idea that such ' Welfare State ' projects as old-age pensions and national insurance on the German model would lead to the decline of the life offices was widespread. In fact, time would show this belief to be utterly misconceived. But, in any case, one would not, in these days, expect to find a Government project of such strong social merit so pointedly criticized in a Salvation Army paper. It illustrates the difficulty experienced by *Assurance* in finding its true role between business on the one hand and the socio-religious motivation on the other.

But these signs of inner conflict were rare, while living Salvationism was abundant. The first issue of *Assurance* carries this example of the dual role of the Salvation Army agent:

> Agent Betts and wife ' specialed ' at Port Brook, the outpost from Malvern, last Sunday night, April 3rd. A most blessed meeting resulted. A little girl led the way to the Penitent-form, soon followed by her mother, and then by her father. There was an indescribable prayer meeting and wind-up. They visited the converts next day; results, 1s. 9½d. worth of good business; again proving that in going for souls, God honours our work.

The best of both worlds, indeed. Elsewhere in the same issue the question was asked:

> Can you make your business a matter of prayer? If not, then give it up.

In 1898 an important new step was taken, the Chief of the Staff, Bramwell Booth, by a General Order declaring the Superintendents and Assistant Superintendents to be officers of The Salvation Army, these titles being equal to those of Adjutant and Captain, respectively. Naturally, *Assurance* made the most of this.

Mr. Gladstone died in 1898 and *Assurance* recalled the Founder's visit to the great man at Hawarden Castle two years earlier. The two men talked of many things, all mainly of a religious nature. Gladstone was friendly and curious, asking many questions about the Army at home and abroad. Only on the question of the Army's leadership did the Liberal statesman express some guarded reservations. He was a democrat to the marrow, but remembered long and painful experiences with dictators—a benevolent autocracy was something not easy for him to visualize. However, he was too polite to argue with his guest. The two men did not discuss life assurance, a subject on which Gladstone could have talked at length.

Chapter
Fifteen

GOOD HEALTH
FOR ALL

OBVIOUSLY, the longer people lived to pay their premiums the better it was for Salvation Army assurance. The Society's magazine, therefore, gave its readers a free medical service, some of which catered for Victorian hypochondria, quackery and superstitions. One wonders, on reading early issues of *Assurance*, whether the paper was not defeating its own ends by killing off the Society's policy-holders. But some of the health hints were merely harmless, as for instance:

> No person should ever eat heartily when very tired. The wisest thing to do is to drink a cup of hot water with three teaspoonfuls of milk in it, sit down for five minutes, and then begin slowly to eat, chewing thoroughly. In a little while the vigour of the stomach will come back, and all will be well.

Readers were told that crushed resin, applied to cuts, would stop bleeding, heal the wound, and ease the pain—at once. Further, they were told that in the opinion of some doctors the use of sulphur in one's boots was effective against influenza. 'Disease cannot exist where there is abundance of pure blood,' one writer asserted. He went on to advocate regular cold baths.

Hydropathy was something of an obsession with the early-day Salvationists. The Founder had found the hydros at Matlock beneficial, following a breakdown, mainly due to dyspepsia. The Army Mother was inclined to place more reliance on quack remedies than on the best of doctors and she had great faith in water-cures. There was a time when any cadet who reported sick at the training garrisons was in danger of being immersed in water to which sulphur, mustard or some other concoction had been added. Early issues of *Assurance* certainly reflected this obsession.

Coffee was not as popular a beverage, in the 1890s, as it is today, but one imagines that many people were shaken by the following indictment which appeared in *Assurance* in 1899:

> The medical director of a life assurance company is reported by *The Philadelphia Ledger* to have stated that coffee-drinking to excess is more injurious to the human system than over-indulgence in whisky. Its effect is in shortening the long beat of the heart, and medical examiners for assurance companies have added the term 'coffee heart' to their peculiar classification of the functional derangements of that organ. These physicians advise that the use of coffee be limited to two cups a day. Coffee topers, they say, are plentiful, and are as much tied to their cups as the whisky toper. The effect of coffee upon the heart is more lasting, and consequently worse than that of liquor.

The cause and cure of the common cold still eludes medical science in the twentieth century but 'Hygea' in *Assurance*, in 1900, was more enlightened:

> A common cold results from blood contamination, occasioned by the retention in the body of effete matter, which should be thrown off through the eight million exhalants (pores) on the body's surface.

The paper championed the Founder's food fad:

> The heart of a vegetarian is said to beat on an average fifty-eight to the minute, that of a meat eater, seventy-two.

The Victorians were notorious for their phobias about fresh air. Tightly shut windows, closed doors and stuffy rooms were considered normal, particularly when sickness was present. *Assurance* is therefore advanced when a woman writer advises:

> A 'healthy exercise' I am happy to recommend, not only because it is possible for nearly every Salvationist to participate in it, but because I can speak from experience of the benefits which it yields, is open-air work. Now, it may not have occurred to you before that any benefit whatever can be derived from this source; but you are wrong if you think so. What is more conducive to constant good health than plenty of pure air? All the time a salvation soldier is present at an open-air meeting she is inhaling fresh air. If she takes an active part in the meetings which she attends, when she speaks or sings, her chest expands, and this not only benefits the lungs, but improves the spirits.

And so the 'health' columns of *Assurance* are used to advance the salvation war.

One of the earliest
Industrial Branch policies

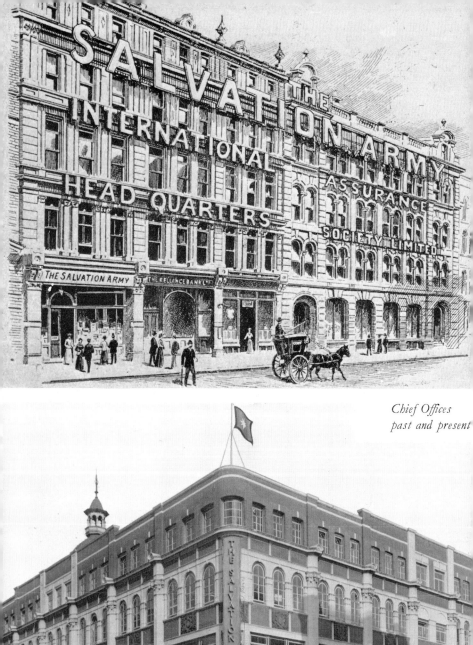

*Chief Offices
past and present*

PRAISE FROM THE CITY

In March, 1899, *Assurance* announced that the new life assurance officers appointed by the Chief of the Staff in 1898 were in need of further regulations. All the Adjutants and Captains were required to complete a local officer's bond and become Envoys. The move was designed to close the gap between the corps and Salvation Army life assurance workers. Brigadier Thomas Marshall, the Head Office Manager reminded the field staff:

> In the first place we must be good soldiers of The Salvation Army, with our names upon the rolls. We cannot be officers unless we are good soldiers. The mere rank or title is a poor empty thing, without the life and reality of consistent soldiership.

The Brigadier went on to claim that headquarters would set a good example:

> The Head Office staff are well to the fore, as becomes their position, with regard to spiritual effort. Numbered among its eighty-four Salvationists are to be found thirteen members of the International Staff Band and sixteen members of the International Staff Songsters. . . . Of corps' institutions, the Penge songsters make the next greatest claim, as fifteen of the Head Office staff are to be found in the ranks of that rising and useful brigade.

This announcement, and others like it at this time, was designed to prevent the rapidly expanding Salvation Army Assurance Society from forgetting that it was an integral part of the Army. Whatever need there may have been for these reminders in some quarters in those far-off days the fervent evangelism and Salvationism of the typical Salvation Army Assurance Society officer was much in evidence.

Not unnaturally *Assurance* gave pride of place to the following announcement, in 1899:

AN EXTRAORDINARY PACE!

From *The Assurance Agents' Chronicle*.

The Salvation Army Assurance Department is shown, by *The Industrial Agents' Guide*, to be still making the pace in an extraordinary manner. The increase in premiums collected places the Army ahead of anything done by any other company or society in 1898. The management expenses have been materially reduced. Under the head of ' Claims, Endowments, and Surrenders,' the experience of the office has been remarkably favourable, only 16.65 per cent. of the total income having been absorbed in this direction. This is a percentage much under that of any other office finding a place in the *Guide*. On the year's working, the very respectable saving of £9,202 has been made, giving a percentage of 13.09, which is over three times better than that of the second largest industrial office in the country, and only falls 3 per cent. short of that of the largest company in the world.

It also announced that Her Majesty Queen Victoria had

purchased several pens of cockerels and pullets from the Salvation Army Farm Colony at Hadleigh. There is no bigotry with Her Majesty.

Perhaps this sign of royal favour was not without influence upon *The Financial Times* which shortly afterwards announced that

> To provide funeral money when a death takes place is an excellent thing, but it is a still more excellent thing to lessen the number of funerals which have to be paid for. The Salvation Army, having entered on the business of industrial life assurance, brings to bear on the problem the practical good sense which marks all its social work. In a neatly got-up twopenny gazette published monthly, which all the representatives have to read and which is largely circulated amongst the members, we find this month an excellent and plainly written article upon infant mortality and how to reduce it, another upon the importance of personal cleanliness, and a third upon the evils of going from the cemetery to the public house to use up any balance of the assurance money. If a readable paper with such contents can be got into the hands of the policy-holders and their wives, backed up by the personal suggestions of the collector on his weekly visits, there is bound to be an improvement which will benefit both the members and the Society. It is ignorance and not want of heart which keeps going the needlessly long procession of small coffins, and this move of The Salvation Army is a likely method of planting the necessary information in the proper place.

At the beginning of Volume 3 of *Assurance*, May, 1900, the same highly influential *The Financial Times* was quoted again in a eulogy which must have been worth a large sum as publicity:

> When The Salvation Army took over the Methodist and General and started to run an industrial life office the whole of the

insurance press was either silent or hostile, and we stood practically alone in our expressed confidence as to the future. Today the institution needs no defender, and it is a pleasure to read its report for last year. In every point it is free from the faults which we so often have to point out in the case of other offices doing similar business. There is no muddling-up of the ordinary and industrial premiums; all the money spent in forming the business is frankly charged to the year's revenue instead of being carried forward as an asset; and yearly the ratio of expenditure is brought down. Practically, the office is only four years old, and we hardly think that any other society of the kind had done so well at the same stage. This is not to be wondered at, for the office has the benefit of the Army machinery, an organization which is nothing short of marvellous. The uniform favourably introduces it to the working class, with no need of explanation or advertisement. Not only are its own direct funds increasing satisfactorily, but it has behind it the whole weight of the Army's assets, pledged by direct guarantee for the security of every policy-holder. The members have a substantial interest in the profits, and the balance of them goes to maintain a good work, the value of which is daily seen by the whole constituency. This being so, the representatives of the institution look for a preference in many quarters, and they are likely to get it in constantly growing measure. It is going to be a big thing, and we wish it the highest degree of success.

The first mass Salvation Army assurance councils, as distinct from sectional gatherings, were held at Clapton on June 5, 6 and 7, 1900. At these the Founder gave what he called his ordination address (see page 12) and Bramwell Booth, the Chairman of the Society, read out the following statement of progress.

FIGURES, PAST AND PRESENT, AS GIVEN IN
THE CHAIRMAN'S OPENING ADDRESS:

Our Life Assurance Department was started in 1894. The premium income was then only £420. In 1895 the premium income in the ordinary branch was £1,131; for 1899, it was £12,862. In the industrial branch, the income in 1895 was £5,860; for 1899, it was £69,256. The assurance effected 250,000 policies in both branches. Claims to end of 1899 have been paid to the amount of £40,524. The Life Assurance Fund has risen from £14,220 to £50,080.

The beginning of the twentieth century, January 1901, found *Assurance* full of confidence in the future. Premium income, after six years of industrial life business, had climbed steadily:

1895	..	.. £5,860
1896	..	.. £18,023
1897	..	.. £35,419
1898	..	.. £50,262
1899	..	.. £69,256
1900	..	.. £80,037

Ordinary branch premium income had risen from £1,131 in 1895 to £16,000 in 1900. The number of policy-holders, wrote Brigadier C. W. Latham, the Chief Accountant, was 219,677 for industrial branch and 5,643 for ordinary branch, with lapsed policies running at a lower rate than ever before.

Expenses, declared the Brigadier,

must necessarily be rather heavy because of the commission, etc., paid for the procuration of new business but our expense ratio is gradually getting less as the following percentage of annual premium income will demonstrate:

1895	..	.. 196.88
1896	..	.. 123.58
1897	..	.. 99.35
1898	..	.. 82.72
1899	..	.. 66.58
1900	..	.. 62.96

He adds a note to the effect that the long-established societies (excluding the Prudential) have average expense ratios of 50 per cent of premium income. The Life Assurance Fund had risen from £14,039 in 1895 to £70,309 in 1900. There were 1,235 agencies, 42 Superintendents, 156 Assistant Superintendents, 3 Inspectors and 111 Head Office officials.

There was an urgent need for men as agents and officers, and this Latham proclaimed in no uncertain terms:

Come over and help us build up a concern that, I venture to say, has no parallel in the history of the world, for never has there been such a combination of enterprising commercialism with aggressive Christianity as exists in Salvation Army life assurance.

As if to emphasize the passing of the old century, and the dawn of the new, *Assurance* gave prominence to the death of Queen Victoria (not omitting mention of the fact that the majestic old lady had insured her life for about £250,000).

In May 1901 *The Financial Times* paid The Salvation Army Assurance Society yet another compliment, part of which read:

> With the whole moral and financial weight of the Army as its guarantor, the office can claim to be as strong as any of the industrial companies, and the time, we believe, is not far distant when the parent organization, instead of having to bear any responsibility, will derive much profit from the established prosperity of its offspring.

A NATIONAL BENEFIT

> The little monthly magazine, *Assurance*, issued by the company, is the best thing of the kind that we have seen, and its wide circulation among the policyholders is positively a national benefit. Clear explanations about life assurance, hints on how to feed the children, medical paragraphs in plain words, readable bits of general information, and a steady interest in the higher life, fill its pages, and make it an indispensable help to the representatives of the company.

Chapter *Seventeen* # EXPANDING YEARS

THE management of Salvation Army life assurance considered itself handicapped by lack of experience. The
expense ratio, for example, was high and numerous be-
ginner's mistakes were being made. The board, therefore,
considered appointing a Mr. Ben Jones, an expert, 'to
develop the business of the Society'. The proposal was not
pursued, probably because of the high salary required, but
the search continued ' for some likely person for Secretary,
from inside one of the life offices', as the minutes put it.
When 75 per cent of profits were allocated for bonuses in
both the industrial and ordinary branches, it was ruefully
noted that ' the Pru' paid out bonuses on 90 per cent of
profits. However, the board took comfort from the fact
that that giant had many years' start.

In March, 1893, ' Life-Giving, London ' was adopted
as the telegraphic address and William Booth, for the Army,
offered £25,000 as capital, ' against such profits as may be
mutually agreed on'. This the board accepted and it
seemed that the new venture was ready to forge ahead.

There was no lack of confidence. In 1894 agents who
were asked to quote for special circumstances, not covered
by Salvation Army tables, were told, ' Quote the same terms
as are given in Prudential tables.' The search for a Secretary,
in place of James Field, who wished to be relieved, went on.
The board still hoped to lure a good man from one of the
leading assurance companies. Though the salary was
hardly tempting—thirty-five shillings—there were 400
applications. But no one was found suitable.

At this time Bramwell Booth gave voice to a proviso
referred to as the ' Foundation Principle ':

> That the poor insurer, who pays his pence for a policy, shall
> have secured to him the same relative facilities in respect of
> surrender values, paid-up policies for lapses, and other equitable
> safeguards, that the rich insurer is entitled to who is able to pay
> his premiums immediately.

This was a standard which could be achieved only by a high degree of commercial success. Could Salvationists achieve it alone?

For a short while it seemed that the unlikely contingency of an ' outsider ' being installed in high place at Head Office was to take place. The board agreed to one Herbert Crook, of the National Life Assurance, Manchester, being accepted to serve for one year at £200 per annum as Assistant Manager, to be increased to £250 for a second year. £5 a week was a large salary in those days, so that it is not surprising that by the next meeting, William Booth, in consultation with Bramwell, had decided against this proposal and the board altered its decision.

The Board of Trade commented adversely on the absence of cash-in-hand in current account. These were small tokens of inexperience but, on January 20, 1894, Major Ernest A. Bremner, the Managing Director, and Mr. Cropper, of the Army's auditors, went along to the country's biggest life office, in Holborn, when ' the Prudential system was explained in the fullest and kindest manner '. The record shows which way the wind was blowing. The Board resolved

> that the best thanks of the Directors are hereby tendered to Board of Directors and Management of the Prudential Life Assurance Company for their courtesy, and kindness in placing most valuable information at the disposal of the Society in its initial endeavour to extend the benefits and blessing of life assurance to the people of The Salvation Army.

Note the limited target, ' to the people of The Salvation Army '. This could be taken to mean to Salvationists, but to Salvationists of those days it meant all people, the poorer people, the great mass of the people embraced by the majestic sweep of William Booth's long arms.

The Army printer quoted £200 for 1,000,000 copies of a new prospectus and, on August 21, 1894, it was decided officially to recruit Superintendents, although some rather haphazard recruitment of individuals had already taken place. The quest was for

Twelve men, as salaried Superintendents for various provincial centres, who themselves will seek and recommend agents for canvassing and act generally as Superintendents.

The Board of Trade again refused permission for the Society to change its rather cumbersome name and also chided the Board for wishing to consist of fifteen Directors. This step, it was pointed out, could be taken only by special resolution of one Extraordinary General Meeting. William Booth, with the Christian Mission experiments in democracy as unhappy memory, was not having any of that and the wish was not pressed.

The first Superintendent in the Society is believed to have been a Major James Ching who, in 1935, was living in retirement at Blackpool. The first agent cannot be named with any certainty, but he may have been Agent A. T. Lee, of Clapton. By 1896 agents and Superintendents were being appointed in considerable numbers and Commissioner Carleton was in firm control. The Society now had a separate existence as an arm of Salvationist endeavour. It had previously been an adjunct of the Property Department and The Salvation Army Bank. It acquired its own officers, recruited its own staff, and waged its own campaigns both commercial and evangelical.

Tea-meetings were arranged for policy-holders, at which the virtues of increased assurance coverage were presented side by side with the claims of the gospel. London was organized into four divisions. Premium income increased by £20,275 in 1897 and more and more provincial offices were opened. It was clear that prejudice against the Society—and Railton had by no means been the sole objector to it—was diminishing. The sincerity and hard work of the ' man on the doorstep ' and the wise administration of Bramwell Booth and his life assurance board of directors proved to be irresistible.

AS THE LAMPS
GO OUT

IN June, 1914, Carleton, blissfully ignorant of the holocaust that was soon to break over Europe, surveyed the progress of the Society. It was an anniversary, for he thought of it as a twenty-year progress: the years of his own term as Managing Director. Bremner's foundation years, the work of James Field and others, from 1891–94, he did not take into account.

The assurance Press had been so laudatory over the 1913 accounts that the Managing Director, familiar with hostile criticism from that quarter, gave warning, ' Woe unto you, when all men shall speak well of you! ' But the 1913 valuation by the Army's consulting actuaries justified satisfaction, as the following figures indicate:

ORDINARY BRANCH

	No. of policies	Sums assured and bonuses			Premiums per annum		
June 30, 1903	8,695	£448,064	3	0	£25,259	13	5
June 30, 1908	22,620	£1,108,833	10	6	£61,688	0	9
June 30, 1913	28,531	£1,531,041	19	4	£77,596	17	5

INDUSTRIAL BRANCH

	No. of policies	Sums assured			Premiums per annum		
June 30, 1903	293,108	£2,996,256	18	6	£122,918	9	8
June 30, 1908	494,623	£5,116,901	10	0	£210,096	2	5
June 30, 1913	648,256	£6,557,618	4	2	£288,225	3	3

In the Society's journal, for the time being called *SAA*, Carleton indulged himself in unwonted pride. June, 1914, was twenty years to the day when the Founder sent for him, to appoint him Managing Director of the ' newly floated ' Assurance Society. His head office staff had been ' one and a half men and a boy '.* Now there were over 300

* In *The Story of The Salvation Army Assurance Society Ltd.*, Lieut.-Colonel John Rivers referred to the staff at this time as ' two men on full-time, one man half-time, and one youth '.

officers and employees. There were over 1,600 agents,
Assistant Superintendents and Superintendents. For them
Carleton used most of the space in his two-page article,
emphasizing the spiritual power of such a salvation force:

> They work hard to earn the bread that perisheth, but I am
> proud to say that they feel it to be a privilege to tell to all they do
> business with, of the Bread of Life. I have heard many beautiful
> stories of backsliders who have wept at the sight of the familiar
> Salvation Army uniform, and who have been faithfully dealt with
> and restored. They pray with the sick and the dying, cheer the
> saints, comfort those who are in trouble or distress, and prove
> veritable messengers of God, bringing the glad tidings of salva-
> tion to the sinner, and hope and consolation to the broken-
> hearted.
>
> It will be seen, therefore, that the Assurance Society has not
> only provided temporal employment for many of our own people,
> but it has also opened up a field for spiritual work which is now,
> and can be increasingly so in the future, of immense service to
> The Salvation Army. The late General often spoke to me of the
> possibilities of advantageous service which can be rendered to
> the Army by the Society, and in his last communication to me
> wrote as follows:
>
> 'All over the land I have been cheered by the assistance
> rendered me by assurance officers. I have found many of them
> most valuable co-workers in my great after-meeting struggles,
> and I can see in this department the possibility of raising a mighty
> force that shall come down with overwhelming effect on the
> devil's kingdom, and take an important part in dealing with the
> miseries with which the world is so crowded.'

He ended his article by pointing out that the assurance funds
were now nearly £1,000,000 sterling, and then, character-
istically, he exclaimed, ' To God be all the glory! '

The review ended with a quote from the *Financial and
Insurance Review*:

> Apart from its connexion with the famous international
> institution, from which it takes its name, and in whose forward
> and uplifting movement it is an integral part, it cannot be said
> that The Salvation Army Assurance Society has bulked largely in
> the public eye. In other words, the Society has gone on from day
> to day quietly achieving and doing its work without the adven-
> titious aid of advertising, and it will come as a shock to many
> people to learn that of all successes during the past few years
> which have been recorded in insurance annals, the greatest is that
> of The Salvation Army Assurance Society. . . .
>
> In life insurance, as in other matters, the old saying that ' merit
> cannot hide itself ' holds good, and there can be no doubt that
> Commissioner Carleton and his staff have accomplished that most

difficult of all tasks—the creation of a life office on lines which render it impregnable to attack and impervious to every contrary influence.

In that year of war Carleton had other grounds for satisfaction. No fewer than fifteen of his Head Office staff entered the Army's training college, among them names to become well known in The Salvation Army: James Ashworth, Frederick Stoker, John Hughes, Rankin Miller, Harry Coote, Charles Cox. Yet as he listed these gains the dark clouds of war were gathering and Britain's Foreign Secretary, Grey, was heard to murmur: ' The lamps are going out all over Europe; we shall not see them lit again in our lifetime.' As if to make the shadows deeper the *Empress of Ireland*, carrying Canadian Salvationists to the great 1914 Congress, foundered in the St. Lawrence, with terrible loss of life.

*SAA*** for September, 1914, lists one officer, one non-officer Assistant Superintendent and twenty-six agents called to the Forces. The officer was one of the first to lose his life. The lists of men called up, and those who volunteered, grew longer, and the Society was soon merging agencies, or arranging for wives to do the work. And in October the first loss in action was recorded, at sea from H.M.S. *Aboukir*—Assistant-Superintendent E. Brumpton. The Society, in common with other life offices, was affected by the Emergency Powers Act, which came into force on August 31. This forbade the lapse of any policy ' without . . . authority of a Court of Justice ', for sums not exceeding £25, and where premiums had been paid for two years prior to August 4, 1914.

Statements in the House, when this act was being argued, hurt Carleton's feelings, for it was said that the companies were ' taking advantage of the present war and the financial difficulties of the poor classes '.

' We do not believe it,' said Carleton, in an article which contained strong criticism of the new act, described by him as ' a good illustration of the evil that may result from hurried legislation '. Of one proviso he wrote: ' It is totally

* A small magazine temporarily replacing *Assurance*.

impracticable and we shall be very surprised to learn that any company takes advantage of it.' Apart from recourse to law, the Act put a heavy burden upon industrial life assurance for an immediate result was that, in most cases, non-payment of premiums could not result in loss of benefit, except by expensive legal action, and this at a time when the newspaper lists of men ' killed in action ' grew longer and longer. In November *SAA* listed claims paid on twenty-one men lost at sea, eleven killed in action on land. Yet this was but the prelude. In December the list of those slain, on whom claims had been paid, filled a whole page of the magazine.

There were happier domestic jottings. An item in the magazine at this time reads:

> We heartily congratulate Assist. Supt. A. F. Grottick, Bedford District, upon his promotion to the rank of Captain.
> The Assistant-Superintendent was a field officer prior to commencing as an agent at King's Cross, on December 31, 1909.
> He was promoted to be Assistant-Superintendent of his present district on January 4, 1913, and has worked hard and produced results which have justified his selection for the position.
> The Captain and his wife are thorough Salvationists, and well respected in the corps and district. We wish them continued success.

When promoted to Glory (aged ninety-seven) Adjutant Grottick was still with The Salvation Army Assurance Society, having given not only his long and devoted service but also three sons—Commissioner William (R.), Lieut.-Colonel Albert (R.), and Lieut-Colonel Wesley, Staff Secretary, National Headquarters.

War cried havoc, and Lieut.-Colonel Braine, the ordinary branch expert at Head Office, did not mince his words:

> Several Assistant-Superintendents will cut a poor figure at the end of the year unless they wake up. Appalling is hardly a strong enough word to define the results secured in some districts. If the comrades referred to have any respect for their reputations they will certainly go in for a good introduction of new business without further delay. Just reflect upon your achievements and ask yourself the question: ' Is this my best ? '
> Eight months of the present financial year have gone, and we stand at a decrease. The matter is very serious. Still, I think we

are well able to remedy this, if everyone makes up his mind to play his part. If each Superintendent would resolve to have from each agent new business each week we should soon begin to see an alteration in things.

But of the pre-war figures, year ending June, 1914, *The Insurance Mail* pays high tribute:

> The Salvation Army Assurance Society closes its year on June 30th, and so its accounts presented herewith do not show any effect of the war. They show just the usual big but steady, sound progress which we have learned by experience to expect from this well-managed office. There is an increase of over 9 per cent in the industrial branch premium income and an increase of over 14 per cent in the ordinary branch premium income. This is really excellent even for a Society which has the proud record of building up a large premium income in a shorter time than any other office. Indeed, we do not trace from the records that The Salvation Army Assurance Society has ever had a better year than the last, for though it has previously issued slightly more new policies in a year, it has never made so large an increase in income. We see with pleasure that the interest earned on the funds has risen appreciably and is now at the rate of over £4 per cent. The industrial branch claims have risen slightly but are still low, and taken in conjunction with an indication of a decreasing lapse rate, speak well for the class of business obtained by the Society. We also note with pleasure that the expense ratio is decreasing notably, and we very warmly congratulate the management on the fact.

But 1915 was a far different story. There were 182 war claims for June alone, while Lord Kitchener's success in gaining volunteers was decimating the ranks of Salvation Army Assurance Society agents. Yet the General Manager, Colonel William Iliffe, was claiming, with probable truth, that no other society had accumulated an Insurance Fund of more than £1,000,000 in so short a period from the date of inception.

Despite the Emergency Powers Act, the Society just held its own. There was not a large accumulation of arrears. All war claims were paid in full although policy conditions could have been operated to the contrary had the Society wished to exercise its option. By November, nearly a thousand men on whom policies had been issued had lost their lives, and the Society had paid out £13,681 19s. od.

There was a grievous shortage of agents yet the Assurance
Fund for the year reached £1,084,569 12s. 9d. By the end
of the year war claims numbered 1,319, with payments
exceeding £16,000.

The number of men killed in action increased steadily
so that, in February, 1916, various escape clauses were
written into ordinary branch and industrial branch, own
life, and life of another policies. From then onwards
monthly lists of war claims were not published, although,
for the year ending June 30, 1916, they amounted to
£18,299. By 1917 the strain on the Society's manpower was
acute. Many women were engaged at Head Office and on
the field. The call-up had ever-lengthening arms as the toll
of dead mounted in Flanders.

Carleton, regular writer in *SAA*, had lost his wife in
1915 and, though he put on a brave face at the time, there
were now undoubted touches of melancholy. He could not
hide his grief, exacerbated by the long lists of dead in the
daily newspapers. His New Year message was hardly cheerful. 'This terrible war,' he wrote, 'this awful carnage!'
Yet the Society was weathering the storm. 'Milestones in
Progress' in *SAA*, January 1917, gave the following
progress report:*

Year	Premium Income			Funds		
	£	s.	d.	£	s.	d.
1894	421	0	0	14,220	0	0
1897	41,376	0	0	28,254	0	0
1900	96,324	0	0	70,309	0	0
1903	136,911,	0	0	154,242	0	0
1906	206,712	0	0	306,630	0	0
1909	262,511	0	0	541,512	0	0
1912	311,170	0	0	800,050	0	0
1915	380,405	0	0	1,084,569	0	0
1916	416,421	0	0	1,207,545	0	0
Total Claims Paid		..	..	£1,315,477		

*Actually, for the last three years given, the Assurance Fund was
in excess of the sums stated.

Chapter Nineteen

UNDER
NEW MANAGEMENT

CARLETON was seventy in May, 1918, and, although much of the supervision of the Society was in the hands of Colonels Iliffe and Cuthbert (the latter having been re-appointed to the Society after the outbreak of war), the Managing Director's regular messages in *SAA*, now a quarterly, leave little room for doubt that he was finding the strain of war, and private grief, heavy upon him. He missed his wife tremendously, and now the war took his second son, William, lost at sea, and three grandsons. The lists of casualties in the daily papers lengthened with every passing day and among them were more and more agents. Conscription was combing the country to meet the insatiable demands of the War Office. To June, 1917, war claims totalled £65,000. Then Iliffe, the General Manager, had a serious nervous breakdown. He had been a prodigious worker but now, to free him from anxiety, it was necessary to release him from his Salvation Army Assurance Society appointment.

In January, 1919, as the post-war era got under way, *SAA* announced that Carleton was retiring. To some this seemed like the end of the world—he had been in charge for twenty-five years, the formative years. No other man would serve so long, or have a greater claim to be considered the ' Father of Salvation Army Assurance '. In his farewell address Carleton revealed that his thirty-eight years of service had all been spent in London, with the exception of about six weeks when he had been in the United States. He had begun as Secretary to Bramwell Booth and they both occupied the same office. In practice, Carleton said, this made him ' Chief Secretary ', ' Field Secretary ', ' Foreign Secretary ' and ' Colonial Secretary ', for there were no others in such posts. He later had charge of Trade, Uniform, and Publishing Departments at the same time. This made him *ipso facto*, Editor-in-Chief, Editor of *The War Cry* and supervisor of *The Young Soldier*, *All the World*, and *The Social Gazette*. Yet probably, in spite of all, he took greater pride in his record as a soldier of Penge Corps. Few men ever had better claim:

> I have had the privilege of being a soldier of one corps for thirty-four years. I have dedicated hundreds of children. I have officiated at over a hundred marriage services—including those of Commissioner Mitchell and Colonel Hurren. I have stood at the graveside of many of our comrades, and wept with those who were in sorrow at the loss of some dear one. I have had some wonderful experiences. I have dedicated thirteen children in one batch in an open-air meeting. I have stood at the graveside and committed the mother's remains to the earth, and in the same service taken the little one that was left behind in my arms, and dedicated him to the service of God; and I am happy and thankful to say that that little one has grown up to be a good and faithful soldier of Jesus Christ. It has been a beautiful experience, and if you only get one-tenth part of the joy and satisfaction from your work as a soldier you will be amply repaid.

Commissioner George Mitchell, the new Managing Director, was one of a new breed of competent Salvationists, reared from boyhood in the Salvation Army fold. Without academic background, he possessed a high degree of intelligence, with a special gift for finance and administration. His arrival at Head Office was followed immediately by a considerable shake-up of staff. Colonel Cuthbert, concluding his second term of service with the Society, departed for Trade Headquarters. Numerous new provincial appointments were made. A few Chief Office men, including Ashworth, were advanced in status. Mitchell soon showed one tactical difference as compared with Carleton, who had not been a great traveller—he took to the road. Councils were held all over the country; Superintendents, Assistants, agents, even agents' wives, attended. The accounts for June 30, 1919, made good reading. The Fund now stood at £1,556,291. Premium income, over £50,000 up on the previous year, was £534,503 for both industrial branch and ordinary branch. Agents were being ' demobbed ', the enlistment of new agents was brisk and there was a scent of new business in the air. The sum of £132,347 in war claims was readily absorbed by the flourishing Society.

There was more money about and agents had their share of it. Lieut.-Colonel Wilfred Acum, who had given the subject special study, wrote on the growing popularity of endowment assurance. Men of thirty, he said, a common age at which assurance policies are taken out, will live another thirty-five years. Many live far beyond. For such men life assurance is more a matter of provision for old age. This was a departure from the traditional ' funeral collecting ' of The Salvation Army Assurance Society, one that would grow in importance as time went by.

It was obvious, from the next accounts, June 30, 1920, that the Society was reaping a rich harvest from the golden post-war years, those deceptive years, when it seemed that Lloyd George's promise would be fulfilled—that Britain would be ' a land fit for heroes to live in '. The Assurance Fund climbed to £1,769,711 5s. 7d. with large increases in premium income and good returns on investments.

In 1920 *SAA* ceased publication. It had lost something of its cheerfulness, becoming very professional in its tone and subject matter. ' Preaching ', and constant admonitions to canvass and do back-calls, were poor substitutes for the *camaraderie* of the old *Assurance* magazine. Also, it seems, the hand of a skilful editor was lacking. Apart from which, Mitchell's constant journeyings, to meet his field personnel all over the country, inclined to make him feel that adequate communication existed.

Then, with the advent of Commissioner William McAlonan to the Managing Director's chair, the unostentatious *Broadcaster* made its appearance, in May, 1923. It was hardly worthy of the Society, now flourishing like the green bay tree. One small sheet, folded into four pages, appearing at irregular intervals, it lacked appeal. The tone was sometimes forbidding—even threatening! As a sample take this full page notice:

INSPECTION

The Managing Director is on ' inspection ' bent.

Look up your dictionary and see what that word means.

Anyhow, there is no doubt in the Managing Director's mind as to what ' inspection ' means, as those who have been already ' inspected ' well understand.

It may happen that he will visit you in the near future.

Should he do so, he will want to see your collecting book, and you will then find out what ' inspection ' means.

There is time for you to ' put your house in order '.

Commissioner McAlonan, a perfectionist, drove the Society with tight rein. One of his early messages was a warning:

Those years [of war], while fruitful in new business, were days of special legislation acting against accuracy in work and records.

Bad habits flourished and now some find it difficult to shake them off.

Well, these bad habits just must be shaken off, for—so far and no farther.

As to the future the watch-word is ' thoroughness and correctness '. . . .

An examination of the work of some agents shows that their errors cannot always be a question of mistake or oversight.

They are more often a matter of sheer, pure, unadulterated carelessness or gross incompetence.

A post-war event that gave great satisfaction to all—except policy-holders concerned—was that the Courts Emergency Act ceased to be operative. A writer in *Broadcaster* noted:

In a few months' time, at the longest, those who have previously sheltered under it will have to face the inevitable. None of the policy-holders who have been protected by it for the last nine years can expect a single further concession. . . . Oh! how glad we shall be when we can see that frightful C.E.A. removed from our collecting books!

Spelling lessons were printed in *Broadcaster* and the general tone of the publication was pedagogical. It is not surprising that at the end of the year it ceased publication.

Chapter Twenty

POST-WAR YEARS

BUT if the magazine languished in the immediate post-war years the Society went on from strength to strength. Premium income and the Assurance Fund rose steeply. The reappearance of *Assurance* gave space for some comparisons:

PREMIUM INCOME

Year ended	Industrial	Ordinary	Combined
June 30, 1908	£191,846	£61,579	£253,425
June 30, 1913	£257,412	£72,209	£329,621
June 30, 1918	£372,391	£109,537	£481,928
June 30, 1923	£558,996	£175,066	£734,062

ASSURANCE FUNDS

Year ended	Industrial	Ordinary	Combined
June 30, 1908	£163,160	£294,080	£457,240
June 30, 1913	£402,047	£479,108	£881,155
June 30, 1918	£736,145	£698,904	£1,435,049
June 30, 1923	£1,573,855	£1,114,880	£2,688,735

At this time *Assurance* began printing Commissioner McAlonan's songs, with music. One of the first, which has survived in general use, is 'All have need of God's salvation', with music by that S.A.A.S. stalwart, Colonel Alfred Braine.

Another innovation was the Salvation Army Assurance Society stand at the Crystal Palace at which the Managing Director and General Manager (Colonel Maxwell) were photographed against the announcement in bold lettering:

ASSURANCE FUNDS EXCEED £3,000,000

SUMS ASSURED EXCEED £16,000,000

A series of visits of Superintendents to London ended in November, 1924, when *Assurance* announced: 'Every Divisional Superintendent in the country has now spent a week at the Chief Office.' The Society's affairs seemed to be progressing most favourably.

But in May, 1925, came the news of the sudden promotion to Glory of the Managing Director. This created an immediate problem for the General, who solved it for the time being by recalling Carleton and making him Joint Managing Director with Colonel Maxwell, who stepped up from General Manager. That post was left unfilled.

If proof were needed that The Salvation Army Assurance Society had now reached the 'First Division', it was provided by the eulogies of the life assurance press and the condolences received from the big life offices: Prudential, Pearl, Refuge, Royal Liver, Britannic, London and Manchester, Royal London, Liverpool Victoria, and others. Some of the Society's pioneers had retired or were about to do so. Brigadier Alex Henderson, Lieut.-Colonel David Wales, Brigadier John Potter, Major A. H. Young, Walter Broom, Geo. Willetts, and others, departed—links with the pioneer days, a fount of self-taught expertise that had been of tremendous value to the Society.

Carleton, with Colonel Maxwell's assistance, took up the reins again with zest. Though he was well past seventy he was still Songster Leader at Penge and able to find time and energy to lead ' away ' week-ends. But by March, 1926, during the great seventieth birthday celebrations of Bramwell Booth, Colonel Maxwell was a Lieut.-Commissioner and Carleton was loosening his hold on the Society for the second time. It was a time of advancement for others. Wilfred Acum, John Spencer, Clifford Grinsted (Reliance Benefit Society) became Colonels, and Joshua Smith a Lieut.-Colonel.

But the clouds of economic decline and industrial unrest were gathering on the horizon. *Assurance* became a quarterly from March, 1926, when a general strike was in the offing. The post-war era of plenty was ending. Agents were warned of the dangers of listening to the radio—a new craze. The listener might not ' hear the business on his own knocker '! In September, 1926, Carleton's second retirement was announced and Lieut.-Commissioner Maxwell took sole charge. The accounts showed substantial advances.

Premium income for 1925 was £833,995 and £437,335 was added to the Assurance Fund which now stood at £3,445,590. A bonus of £2 per cent per annum was declared for policy-holders.

The eulogies of the financial and assurance Press were now a matter of course and the 1925 figures were no exception. One rather unusual tribute appeared in the *Assurance Review*.

> The career of The Salvation Army Assurance Society has been one long and uninterrupted triumphal march. Like the Army itself, this Assurance Society has known its days of trial and tribulation. Like the Army itself, it has never known a check in its progress. . . .
>
> The Salvation Army Assurance Society does not only collect premiums from its members in their brighter days, but it distributes benefits to them when the shadows fall and the brighter days seem to have passed.
>
> It enters the homes of the people when the blinds are drawn and the hearts are broken. What can be done to assuage the grief and lighten the sorrow it does as, perhaps, no other organized body can do. With its tender touch and its story of the Cross it comes, and not empty-handed, but with the means of making material things easier for the suffering souls. That is part of the work of The Salvation Army Assurance Society, and that alone will supply a very good reason for the wonderful success the Society has had ever since The Salvation Army has had control of its doings and its destiny.

Lieut.-Commissioner Maxwell's term in sole charge of The Salvation Army Assurance Society was brief. The January, 1927, number of *Assurance* contained news of his appointment as Territorial Commander for the Canada East Territory. Lieut.-Commissioner William J. Haines was appointed to succeed him. Haines was a Salvationist financier, having come all the way from International Headquarters office boy through various posts which included terms as Director of The Salvation Army Assurance Society; Director, Reliance Bank; Director, Salvation Army Fire Insurance Corporation; and Trustee, Reliance Benefit Society. His time at The Salvation Army Assurance Society was also to be short—tragically so. Yet his impact on the Society was dramatic. Reorganization and modernization became the order of the day.

At this time the Society seemed to show a greater awareness of ordinary branch assurance—the assurance of the future. Pressure to develop this less expensive 'better class' sort of business is noticeable in the magazine and in the pep talks of Chief Office executives. 'How Agent Christie of Coleraine Secured his £1,000 Case' is the heading of an article published in January, 1927, and there were many similar encouragements. Later in the year one agent, at Leyton, sent in proposals for £6,500 in one week—a record to that date.

In passing, *Assurance* noted, in January, 1927, that Commissioner Carleton had relinquished the baton as Songster Leader at Penge—but he remained Chairman of the Board of Directors of The Salvation Army Assurance Society. In the same year a whole column was devoted to the promotion—to the rank of Major—of one Ernest Wellman, the Society's Secretary, who was already 'a valuable asset', possessor of 'an extensive and growing knowledge of the manifold ramifications of life assurance'.

The accounts for 1926 reflected something of the hard times afflicting the country. The rate of growth was not sustained. But the Fund was increased by £297,960 and a bonus of £2 2s. was declared on all participating policies. During 1927 there was partial economic recovery and the Society forged ahead. There was still no General Manager but the Field Manager, newly promoted Colonel William McCarthy, carried out many of the duties of the vacant post.

In 1928 *Assurance* was back to monthly publication, with Brigadier John Rivers as the new editor. A training scheme for would-be Superintendents was announced, and twelve districts joined to make a special London Division, with Brigadier William T. Adams in charge, and Staff-Captain Percy Mayor as second in command.

For the first time, to any extent, the law, procedures and Army policy on investments were explained at Swanwick Councils (also published in *Assurance*) by Brigadier Railton Howard, the Chief Office expert. These investments now totalled over £4,000,000 and were a side of the business to be very carefully watched and attended to ' because it is one of the sources from which the Society obtains the where-withal to pay that £2 2s. bonus '.

In 1928 a well-known Army assurance pioneer, Lieut.-Colonel Joseph Reardon, was reappointed to Chief Office. He had been on special missions for the General and while in Australia he had conducted a survey on the possibility of opening up The Salvation Army Assurance Society in that country.

There had already been investigations as to the possi-bility of the Society branching out in the United States. But it was not to be. Legal, social and manpower problems proved insuperable. The Salvation Army Assurance Society remained a British concern, but very progressive. In January and February, 1928, fifty-five new agents were appointed. Income soared while the Managing Director stirred things up by a wide change of Divisional Managers, all of whom were given public installations led by the Commissioner.

The 36th Report, 1927, showed all-round increases. £320,114 was added to the Fund, which now stood at £4,240,491. A bonus of £2 2s. was again declared. Com-missioner Carleton, still attending to his duties as Chairman, was eighty on May 21st, and ' a small band ', ' a number of singers ' and representative officers from Chief Office staff serenaded their Chairman from the lawn of his house in Queen Adelaide Road, Penge. The Managing Director read the 91st Psalm. He was so young, compared with Carleton, so tall and vigorous. He would have seemed to be a good risk for a life assurance policy.

From 1928 the magazine *Assurance* had a bright new look about it. This was not only because of the dynamic and extraordinarily active leadership of Lieut.-Commissioner Haines but also because of the skilled, bookish and broad-minded John Rivers, the editor, who set a new standard for the paper. There was some hard-hitting:

Out of the quite respectable number of agents representing

the Society during the last financial year a mere three dozen
accomplished really good results in either branch. . . .
    Life assurance is a man's job. . . . Judging by what we both see
and hear we incline to the idea that many quacks are engaged
therein. . . . If you can't do a job, say so!

At the end of 1928 another sign of the growing strength
and respectability of The Salvation Army Assurance Society
was seen when six of the leading British banks agreed to
cash cheques drawn by the Society on the Reliance Bank.
The Salvation Army Assurance Society seemed to be riding
on the crest of the wave.

But 1929 began catastrophically. In January the Chairman, octogenarian Carleton, called the staff together at Chief
Office to tell them that their Managing Director had been
suddenly promoted to Glory, from Sunbury Court, where
he had been elected Vice-President of the High Council then
in session. In a short time Lieut.-Commissioner Haines had
made a unique mark on the Society. He had shown great
gifts as a business executive; he was beloved for his care over
all who worked for the Society, both employees and officers.
Unable to find accommodation, many hundreds were
turned away from the funeral service, led by the Chief of
the Staff, at Clapton Congress Hall.

With the appointment of Lieut.-Commissioner David
Cuthbert to be its Managing Director the Society can be
said to have stepped out of history into recent times, for the
Commissioner remained at the helm until the eve of the
Second World War. He was himself an old Salvation Army
Assurance Society man, having been first appointed to the
Society in 1895, and was its General Secretary when he left
it in 1912. One of his first tasks was to tackle the formidable
Daily Express, which had issued a damaging statement on
the Army's use of Assurance Society funds. It was, of
course, a time for sensational Press publicity, the period
following the first High Council. But the paper apologized
and in no half-hearted fashion:

    There is no foundation for the statement that £70,000, or any
sum, has been advanced to the general funds of The Salvation
Army by the Directors of The Salvation Army Assurance Society,

Ltd., to enable the routine work of the various London head-quarters to be carried on. No such proposal has even been under consideration, and the *Daily Express* regrets the publication of the erroneous report.

The 1928 accounts show that premium income was just short of the million and that the Fund had risen to £4,357,331. A bonus of forty-four shillings per cent of sums assured was declared. Though the ' big slump ' was just around the corner and economic stringency was already evident, the upward climb of the Society continued.

In June, 1929, General Bramwell Booth answered the Home-call. It was another broken link with the first days. He had been the chief agent in the formation of the Society, first its Chairman, and then President to the end. His superb business organization, his vision of what the Society could become, had carried the venture forward from its small beginnings. He, more than any other individual, was responsible for the meticulous regard for spiritual values: The Salvation Army Assurance Society was to be no mere money machine. It was Bramwell Booth who had given The Salvation Army Assurance Society its daring, awe-inspiring credo—' Holiness unto the Lord—that is our trade mark.' He saw the Society align itself with that high standard, and always he lived the life of holiness himself.

*Chapter
Twenty-one* # THE MEN IN CHARGE

EXCEPT for Major Ernest A. Bremner, the first Managing
Director of the embryo Society, all the men appointed to the
leading position in The Salvation Army Assurance Society
held the rank of Commissioner or were promoted to it
shortly after their appointment. With one or two exceptions
they were all 'imported', coming into the Society from
'outside'. Although, in theory, this handicap should have
been ruinous it worked very well. It was, after all, an
expression of the Salvationist adaptability shown in other
fields of service, and one imagines that here it enabled the
General to infuse new blood and new methods into the top
echelon of the Society.

Exceptions to the rule, in which officers with more or
less lengthy experience of life assurance were appointed
from inside the Society, were Commissioners Maxwell and
Cuthbert, and the present Managing Director, Commissioner William Villeneuve.

In chronological order the men in charge were:

Major Ernest A. Bremner (1891–1894)

Commissioner John A. Carleton (1894–12.2.1919)

Commissioner George Mitchell (20.2.19–15.11.21)

Commissioner William J. McAlonan (16.11.21–1.5.25)

Commissioner John A. Carleton (jointly, 13.5.25–24.6.26)
    and Colonel William Maxwell

Commissioner William Maxwell (24.6.26–12.11.26)

Lieut -Commissioner William J. Haines (13.11.26–
    18.1.29)

Commissioner David Cuthbert (4.4.29–30.12.37)

Commissioner David Cuthbert (jointly, 30.12.37–
    and Commissioner Charles Baugh   31.10.38)

Commissioner Charles Baugh (31.10.38–30.9.43)

Commissioner Frank Dyer (30.9.43–3.2.51)

Commissioner Ranulph M. Astbury (5.2.51–28.1.56)
Commissioner Hugh P. Muir (28.1.56–30.12.61)
Commissioner William A. Villeneuve (1.1.62–   )

From Office Boy

George Mitchell was probably the first International Headquarters office boy to reach the rank of Commissioner. If this is so it is remarkable, for he was by no means the kind of lad who modelled himself on Smiles's *Self Help*, a popular and improving textbook of those times. On at least one occasion young Mitchell was given a week's notice by a despairing Staff Department at International Headquarters. But he was not easily disposed of, nor was his ascent to high places long delayed. He quickly developed into a good business man, serving in a variety of financial posts, displaying the high standard of business acumen which was to make him first the Army's Chancellor of the Exchequer, and then the Managing Director of The Salvation Army Assurance Society.

This great progress, in the tradition of *Log Cabin to White House*, from office boy to the Chancellor's chair, Mitchell made in twenty-eight years. It was combined with the heavy duties of an active public life, which included wielding the baton of the International Staff Band; he was its Bandmaster for twenty-five years. Other appointments included that of Territorial Commander for Sweden, and International Secretary at International Headquarters, during which time he visited the United States, Canada, India, China and Korea. Though he could concentrate on numerous problems he always took them one at a time, showing remarkable ability to master a new subject. He could turn from life assurance to the Staff Band practice and give that engagement his whole mind and heart; when he stood on a street corner to proclaim the news of salvation men felt, ' Here is a man who really cares about what happens to me '. He was noted for his coolness under pressure. His strong personality was always kept under strict discipline. He was a typical 'success story' of late Victorian times, a Commissioner at forty-five, but quite unspoiled by success. He remained modest, sympathetic and approachable. Only those who gave less than their best, cynics and idlers, felt the power of his tongue, and that was formidable indeed. In his prime he was easily the outstanding figure in the Army's musical world yet maintained a dynamic spiritual impact through all. His term as Managing Director was from February, 1919, to November, 1921. He was promoted to Glory in 1930.

Song-writer

Commissioner William J. McAlonan had charge of the Society from November, 1921, to May, 1925, when he was suddenly promoted to Glory. For some years he had suffered from a serious heart condition and it is said that in the knowledge of this, at the end of every day, he ordered his affairs in readiness for the final summons.

Converted at Ligoniel, in Northern Ireland, as a young officer he soon displayed studiousness, talent and devotion, gaining rapid promotion. He served as Chief Secretary in Britain, and as Territorial Commander for Germany, Sweden, the Netherlands and Switzerland, then as International Secretary, in which capacity he visited the Far East, Africa and other lands. He had a warm missionary zeal and took pride in the fact that part of Salvation Army Assurance Society profits was allocated to missionary work. Writer of ' I have seen His face in blessing ' and 'All have need of God's salvation ', he was also a gifted linguist and possessed a remarkable memory. Carleton, ' father ' of the Army's Assurance Society, was his mentor as a young officer. They were both from the same district near Belfast. McAlonan was Carleton's assistant at the Clerkenwell Trade Headquarters. The Society was making splendid headway under his control and his premature passing at the age of sixty-two was truly described as a calamity.

A Short Term

Commissioner William Maxwell served as Joint Managing Director with Commissioner Carleton from May, 1925, to June, 1926, following the sudden passing of Commissioner McAlonan. He remained as Managing Director from June to November, 1926.

He entered into officership from Dundee in 1894 and then commanded various corps. Later he became Under Secretary for European Affairs at International Headquarters. His short term in charge of the Society was followed by a period as Territorial Commander for Canada East and then for Southern Territory, Australia. He later became Head of Salvationist Publishing and Supplies, Limited, and Principal of the International Training College, from which appointment he retired in 1946. He was promoted to Glory in 1953.

Dynamic Quality

Lieut.-Commissioner William J. Haines, C.B.E., was promoted to Glory on January 18, 1929. He had been Managing Director of The Salvation Army Assurance Society since November, 1926. He entered the Army's service from Camberwell, in 1888, and began work in the International Headquarters Post Office as a boy of fourteen. He became an officer in 1891, remaining at International Headquarters until 1895, when he was appointed to Norway. There he remained for nine years, developing a keen business aptitude in his work in the Finance, Property and Trade Departments. At the outbreak of the First World War he was Finance Secretary in Germany, where he had served for ten years. Having to leave the country hurriedly he then became responsible for war work among the troops in France. For this service he received both Belgian and British decorations. After the war he served in the Finance Department of International Headquarters, being Finance Secretary when he was appointed to The Salvation Army Assurance Society.

His term of control of the Society was just time enough
to hint at the dynamic quality of the man. He organized the
office canteen and made a rule ' that offices should be
vacated and aired every lunch hour '.* He was serving as
Vice-President of the first High Council at the time of his
sudden passing, at Sunbury Court. He was in his fifty-
fourth year.

A Scholar

David Cuthbert had boyhood ambitions to be a jour-
nalist and, in the Army, he showed proof of a gift for
writing. But his ambition to be a full-time editorial worker
was never realized. He was converted as a boy at Perth and
as a young convert helped to form a Salvation Mutual
Improvement Society, a project that does not seem so odd
in a young Scot. His idea of a pleasant, free Saturday
afternoon was a walk in the country, studying the Bible as
he went.

After a time at Glasgow Headquarters he became, in
1889, secretary to Commissioner Carleton, who was then
in charge of the Army's publishing affairs. He was appointed
to Salvation Army assurance in 1895 and remained there
until 1912, making a mark on the Society as a prolific and
well-informed writer in *Assurance*, *The Officer* and the *Staff
Review*. He also became a gifted public speaker, a theologian,
an efficient life assurance worker, the Society's Cashier and
the first General Secretary. Appointments at Salvationist
Publishing and Supplies, Limited (after a second period
with the Society during the First World War), as Director
of Emigration, and at Hadleigh Farm Colony followed, the
Commissioner becoming Governor of the latter centre in
1924. He was a scholar with a wide range of reading and an
inquiring mind. But he also interested himself in people
who, despite his rather austere demeanour, liked and
respected him. He became Managing Director of The
Salvation Army Assurance Society in 1929, remaining in

* *The War Cry*, January 26, 1929.

charge until he retired in 1938. His policy for the Society was expansionism and he initiated the appointment of leading officers of the Society to directorships. He saw premium income go well past the million mark annually, an unimagined rise from the meagre sums of his early days. In 1895, his first year with the Society, premium income totalled £6,992. He was promoted to Glory in 1953.

Became Chief of the Staff

It is part of Salvation Army history that Charles Baugh, at the age of one year, helped to quell the activities of toughs who tried to disturb the meetings led by his parents in Whitechapel in the days of the ' Skeleton Army '. His mother arranged for the malcontents to nurse him and the official history records that as they passed him from one to the other, in the meetings, ' the Baugh baby played no small part in winning them over '. One of the gang of hoodlums, thus pacified and later converted, became Commissioner Charles Jeffries.

Charles Baugh went to International Headquarters as a schoolboy and was placed in the Accountant's Department, later becoming a member of the International Staff Band. At the outbreak of the First World War Major Baugh was appointed to Simla, the then headquarters of the India and Ceylon Territory. Later, when India was divided into separate commands, he became Chief Auditor for all, with Ceylon added. In the course of his duties he travelled from Poona to Ceylon, a journey of 3,000 miles, five times in eighteen months. In 1926 he became Territorial Commander for Northern India, with responsibility for criminal tribes. The settlement of criminal tribes in the Andaman Islands was brought about at this time.

He became Auditor-General at International Headquarters in 1930 and then Joint Managing Director of The Salvation Army Assurance Society in 1937, assuming full control of the Society in 1938. From 1943 to 1946 he was Chief of the Staff to General Carpenter. Command of Canada followed until 1951, when the Commissioner retired. Two

years later he was promoted to Glory. He had married
Ensign Nellie Stewart in 1906.

Able Administrator

Commissioner Frank Dyer, who, as a junior of Clapton
Congress Hall, was chosen to represent the young people's
corps at the funeral of the Army Mother, was another of
that galaxy of men who began their Salvation Army service
at International Headquarters. He began work there at the
age of fourteen. In great part the benefit of this background was the shared experiences with the greathearts who
were to be found there: William and Bramwell Booth,
Railton, Howard. . . . In Frank Dyer's case, while engaged
in secretarial work, there was the glorious privilege of
sharing family prayers with the Founder's household at
Hadley Wood. He was also greatly influenced, while serving
in the Auxiliary Department, by Commissioner Randolph
Sturgess. As an officer Dyer gained knowledge of needy
men and social administration at the Hadleigh Farm Colony.
Later he crossed and recrossed the Atlantic as an assistant
in Commissioner David Lamb's Migration Department.
After a period as Under Secretary in one of the International
Headquarters Overseas Departments, he became Director
of The Campfield Press where, for fifteen years, he showed
highly competent, unfussy ability as an administrator.

There was a term as International Secretary for the
British Dominions, the Americas and Europe, and then, in
1943, he became Managing Director of The Salvation Army
Assurance Society. It might have been expected that he
would be the perfect business machine, the human com-
puter, the cool, efficient business man, for all his Salvation
Army life had been spent on staff work. But he remained at
heart the simple Salvationist, a plain man, modest, unspoiled, his spiritual life uneroded by material affairs. He
attended the corps at Harpenden, and for some years was
Songster Leader there. His term as Managing Director
included the trying days of the Second World War and the

Above: The Assurance Songsters
Below: Rosehill Band

PIONEERS

First Chairman,
General
W. Bramwell Booth

General
William
Booth

Founder of
The
Salvation
Army

Commissioner
John Carleton

struggle for reconstruction that followed after. When he retired, in 1951, the Society had, under his leadership, weathered the storms of war and shared in that boom of life assurance that marked the late 1940s. He was promoted to Glory in 1957.

Junior Clerk to Managing Director

Commissioner Ranulph Astbury, who became Managing Director of The Salvation Army Assurance Society, was converted as a schoolboy at Stoke Newington Corps, London. When his parents became officers he began that wide knowledge of The Salvation Army that was to serve him in good stead in the years to come. He became a junior clerk on International Headquarters, that cradle in which so many leading officers of the future were nourished. Entering training in 1904, he had a period of corps work and was then appointed to Provincial Headquarters at Glasgow. Various headquarters appointments followed, including Finance Secretary at International Headquarters and a directorship of The Salvation Army Assurance Society. While Auditor-General he took charge of the International Training College, holding both responsibilities for more than twelve months. After two years in charge of the Men's Social Services the Commissioner was appointed in 1946 as Territorial Commander for New Zealand, and in 1951 succeeded Commissioner Dyer as Managing Director of The Salvation Army Assurance Society—a post he filled until his retirement in 1956. He was promoted to Glory in 1968.

A Not-So-Ordinary Man

Commissioner Hugh Muir once described himself as a ' very ordinary man '—and that is the impression one was likely to receive at first acquaintance. There is nothing striking about his appearance and, as he is essentially a modest man, erroneous first impressions are likely. But, despite his own evaluation, Hugh Muir is quite out of the ordinary. He has made a much-above-average contribution

D—A.U.S.

to the *morale* and progress of The Salvation Army Assurance Society.

Hailing from Twechar, in Dunbartonshire, he absorbed a great deal of Scottish Presbyterianism, including Old Testament history and general Bible knowledge, from a young Presbyterian minister. This helped to develop his spiritual life and make him an arresting speaker. After he became an officer, and had served some time on corps work, his considerable gifts as an administrator were discovered by the Army and used to very good effect in one executive position after another. These included the Men's Social Services, Hadleigh Farm Colony, Salvationist Publishing and Supplies, Limited and, finally, The Salvation Army Assurance Society.

It is, of course, ' unprofessional ' that a non-assurance man should be put in executive control of an assurance society, but the Army has long been a law unto itself in such matters and, though Hugh Muir is not the only instance of this adaptability, he is certainly an outstanding example of it. Measured by Army experience of transferring men from one kind of work to another, and judged by the successful ' reign ' of Commissioner Muir as Managing Director, the modern cult of specialization may not have so much to commend it as many people assert.

Hugh Muir brought to The Salvation Army Assurance Society a knowledge of people and a marked ability to understand them and mix with them, employees and officers alike. He displayed a genuine interest in their life and problems and never practised that doctrine of ' splendid isolation ' felt by some to be a necessary concomitant of executive authority.

During his six years as Managing Director the funds of the Society increased by £5,000,000 and many improvements were made in salaries and conditions of service of the assurance staff. One of the outstanding achievements for which the Commissioner will be remembered by agents was the establishment of a non-contributory pension scheme with provisions for widows' pensions.

The Commissioner retired at the end of 1961, leaving the Society in a very healthy condition, with prospectuses modernized, and premium income and investment income increased. Yet the spiritual and social objectives of Salvationist life assurance were always kept well to the fore. One feels that unless this were so then Hugh Muir would have no part in it.

He Challenged God

Commissioner William A. Villeneuve, the present Managing Director, took charge of the Society in 1962. From 1920 to 1946 he had been a missionary in India and Burma, twenty-six years that might seem to have been wasted from the point of view of one who was to become an assurance society executive. But it has often been the case in The Salvation Army that overseas service contributes something to a man's career that enhances his fitness for high responsibility. Though he did not know it, service in India was preparing William Villeneuve for his future. There were appointments as Finance Officer and Financial Secretary on the one hand, and on the other a term as Divisional Commander and the appointment to the control of a Red Shield centre during the Second World War. There, hundreds of men on leave from the Burma jungle battles found rest, food and good fellowship at the centre run by Major and Mrs. Villeneuve. So business training and the ability to mix with men, and understand their problems, were part of the reward of the years in India which came to William Villeneuve as he began his duties at Chief Office.

The son of a pioneer Divisional Manager of the Society, William Villeneuve entered training in 1920, from Pontypridd, in South Wales. His father used to tell the story of his son's impediment of speech; of how, as a cadet, he asked God to remove the disability that hindered the word. Like Isaiah, of another time, he challenged God—'If you are calling me to serve You, then touch my lips that I may

D*—A.U.S.

speak.' God accepted the challenge. When William Villeneuve sailed for India there was no stutter, nor is there now.

In 1946 Major Villeneuve became the Accountant at The Salvation Army Fire Insurance Corporation and in due course Chief Accountant at The Salvation Army Assurance Society. A term as General Manager followed and, in January, 1962, his appointment as Managing Director. It should be noted that though he had been twenty-six years abroad the rest of the years had been spent with the Society.

Chapter Twenty-two

THEY OPENED
THEIR MOUTHS

SONGS were sung from the first by those who launched and developed Salvation Army assurance. Small groups of agents, led by a Superintendent, conducted meetings in which salvation was the main theme with ' new business ' as the postscript. The war songs of The Salvation Army accompanied all. On headquarters, especially when Carleton was at the helm, singing had a premier place, and singing brigades took part in official headquarters gatherings and field campaigns. The International Staff Songsters had an illustrious career under Colonel Herbert J. Jackson, himself an Army assurance ' tycoon '. He was the leader for twenty-five years. There were numerous members of the Assurance Society personnel in the International Staff Band.

To a large extent the place of the Staff Songsters was taken by the Assurance Songsters. The leader was Brigadier Railton Howard, who was to hold the baton for twenty years. He took the brigade to very high standards of excellence. Public operations began at Leicester in June, 1928, a ' provincial run ', with the Managing Director, Lieut.-Commissioner Haines, in charge.

Fifteen hundred people were at the Regent Hall the following September for the first London festival in which the brigade took part. There were 250 Army assurance musicians: a Chief Office band, with fifty members; a field band, with ninety; a concertina band and a Chief Office boys' band—' a Musical Panjoram ' Lieut.-Commissioner Haines called it. *The Bandsman and Songster* critic wrote that the new songster brigade produced some ' fine *ppp* and *pppp* effects too seldom heard from Army vocalists '.

Lieut.-Commissioner Haines, a great innovator, shook up many of the settled ways of The Salvation Army Assurance Society. Founding the Assurance Songsters was one among many of his creative acts. When he was so suddenly promoted to Glory one of the brigade wrote of him: ' What an example of out-and-out Salvationism he was to us all! ' Indeed, as if in emulation of the Commissioner's soul-saving zeal, the brigade showed by many a salvation campaign, all over Britain, that its chief interest was not to display its undoubted vocal virtuosity but to win men and women for God.

It did duty at the lying-in-state of General Bramwell Booth, in 1929, and among highlights of its ministry can be mentioned national Bandmaster's councils, when the brigade demonstrated points in Brigadier Howard's lecture, ' Salvation Song ', and a ' Northern Tour ' in Manchester, Oldham, Liverpool and Southport, with Commissioner and Mrs. Cuthbert as leaders. This occasioned a week away from office duties.

So many great occasions are on record in the history of the Assurance Songsters that selection is difficult. The festival given in the speech room at Harrow public school, in September, 1930, was certainly a great occasion. In his tribute, the Head, Dr. Cyril Norwood, said: ' The secret of the Army's power lies in its firm grip on the foundation of religion. That foundation is love! The attitude of the world toward the Army has changed because it has shown the world that the doctrine of love is not a mere theory—wherever there is sorrow and suffering there you will find the Army busy! '

In June, 1931, the height of the ' slump ' in Britain, the brigade did a ten-day campaign in Scotland and were billed in a Dundee paper as the ' Famous Salvation Army Choir '. Commissioner Cuthbert led in meetings held at Stirling, Aberdeen, Dundee, Perth, Edinburgh, Paisley, Kilmarnock, Clydebank and Glasgow. If office duties were neglected during this long absence, one imagines that compensation was gained from publicity and goodwill for the Society. There is no evidence of any decline in business though one can imagine the reactions of executives of any other life assurance company if the Managing Director and about forty members of the staff took ten days off to go on an evangelistic campaign!

In 1931 the singing of the brigade attracted a crowd somewhere in the interior of China, whence Ensign James Gilman wrote to Lieut.-Colonel Howard of the recordings, 'Jesus, Thou art everything to me' and 'Jesus said, I am the resurrection', the brigade's first disc. 'This is easily the best that the Army has turned out,' said the Ensign. The price of the record, incidentally, was 1s. 6d.

A choir-master at Luton, after hearing the brigade, went to his own church to say to his choir: 'I wish you had been with me last night. I am always telling some of you girls to open your mouths wider. Those songsters do know how to open their mouths.'

In 1934 another great occasion for the brigade was the farewell of General and Mrs. Higgins, at the Royal Albert Hall. H.R.H. the Duke of York presided, accompanied by the Duchess. The brigade sang, 'I'll stand for Christ', 'preserving its warmth and simplicity, without losing anything of the stateliness of a royal occasion', as *The Bandsman and Songster* put it. In 1935 General Evangeline Booth attended the brigade practice and rehearsed the singing of her new song, 'My longing heart'. Among the particularly warm admirers of the brigade, because of its vocal excellence and the skill of its leader, was Sir Dan Godfrey, the well-known Bournemouth Municipal conductor.

The brigade was at the height of its powers when the Second World War created administrative chaos. The Salvation Army Assurance Society removed itself to 'Rosehill', near Reading, and the brigade, with its members divided between London and Reading, could not function. However, an 'interim brigade' was soon formed, which took part in holiness meetings at Reading Central Corps, led by the Managing Director, Commissioner Baugh. This group visited various military camps and numerous corps and central gatherings.

Shortly after the end of the Second World War Colonel Howard retired, having made a unique contribution to The Salvation Army Assurance Society, not only in music, but in various financial posts. His final appointment was as

General Secretary. With the Colonel's going it somehow seemed fitting that the brigade should be disbanded. It passed into the Army's musical history, full of triumphs and hallowed memories, in 1947.

Chapter
Twenty-three THE ROSEHILL BAND

INEVITABLY, instrumental music made early appearance at
the Chief Office of The Salvation Army Assurance Society.
As brass bands became an integral part of Salvationist
endeavour, and as the number of men employed by the
Society increased, there was soon a host of players in
hundreds of corps whose week-day occupation was Salvation Army life assurance. But the first Assurance Society
band, as such, came in 1928, at a heyday in Salvation Army
musical history, when the Society put 500 musicians into
one festival, presided over by the musically minded Lieut.-
Commissioner Haines.

The Assurance Band of fifty players took part under the
baton of Bandmaster Fred Buckman, renowned cornetist
with the International Staff Band. Society employees in The
Salvation Army Assurance Society's combination included
Geoffrey Dalziel, Arthur Hook, Cyril Brisley and Bernard
Adams, all of whom later became members of the Inter-
national Staff Band, the latter its Bandmaster. This Salvation
Army Assurance Society band marched in the Lord Mayor's
Show, the first time the Army took part in this annual event.
The Lord Mayor was Sir Kynaston Studd, one of the famous
cricketing brothers, who, like the more famous C.T., dis-
played a warm interest in the Army.

The Chief Office Band gave way to the Assurance Headquarters Boys' Band, directed by Henry Nott. In time the
word 'Boys' was omitted from the title and, as the Assurance Headquarters Band, the section took part in the 1939
Associated Headquarters Festival at the Clapton Congress
Hall.

The Second World War extinguished three of the headquarters bands, as it did so much else. But it called another
band into being—the most notable Salvation Army Assurance Society band. When the bombing of London caused
business houses to evacuate the city, the Society took refuge

in 'Rosehill', a large country house near Reading, that had been, among other things, a Roman Catholic School.

Down there men employees and officers were cut off from their own corps activity, which, for many, meant a place in the band. So a band was formed, called 'Rosehill', with Major Walter Ward as its first Bandmaster. Ward was a first-class conductor, Bandmaster of the Cambridge Heath Band and solo cornetist with the International Staff Band. For the new Salvation Army Assurance Society unit he had excellent material before him. Proof of this came in about six months, when the B.B.C. invited the band to an audition, which was soon followed by an engagement to broadcast. Throughout the war, despite the loss of men to military service, the band maintained a high standard, alternating with the International Staff Band in presenting manuscript music for the International Music Board.

For a short while, in 1942, the incomparable Eric Ball was Bandmaster, passing on, after only a few months, to become International Staff Bandmaster. Colonel Albert Jakeway succeeded him, and nowadays this name, more than any other, is conjured up when Rosehill is mentioned. Colonel Jakeway took the band to high standards of performance, enriched as it was by the return of Service men who were highly gifted instrumentalists. Indeed, from the first, Rosehill's high standards of performance owed much to its ability to recruit men who were virtuosos.

But, like other Headquarters bands, and the Assurance Songsters, Rosehill Band passed into history, ceasing to function in 1951. This was a time of post-war reconstruction, and also a boom period in life assurance. A famine of staff, and extreme pressure of work, made it more and more difficult to find time and manpower.

Chapter Twenty-four

A UNIQUE SOCIETY

THE SALVATION ARMY ASSURANCE SOCIETY is still largely a
society geared to the week-by-week, house-to-house
collection of premiums, though some life assurance offices
have already ceased to issue policies on a weekly premium
basis. There is little doubt that this is the trend for the
future.

A reason for the shift of emphasis is that the cost of
week-by-week collection is relatively high, while it is
undeniable that many workers now have the money, and
the habits of thrift, which enables them to pay for their
assurance policies at quarterly, half-yearly or even annual
intervals. This makes possible a lower expense ratio and a
more remunerative return for the policy holder.

Yet The Salvation Army Assurance Society, despite
the attractive economics of ' cheque book ' life assurance,
remains a unique society because of the fact that its main
concentration is and will continue to be industrial branch
life assurance—that is, the door-to-door weekly collection
of premiums. The latest set of figures (1967) shows clearly
where the emphasis lies: ordinary branch premium income,
£814,941; industrial branch, £2,353,617. In most societies
nowadays ordinary branch premium income is overtaking
and often exceeding that of the industrial branch.

William Booth was an ordinary branch client himself,
£21 annually, but he knew that to the mass of Britons this
sort of life assurance was out of the question. He saw his
agent as the man who collected the premiums every week.
This would enable him to be a friend of the family as well as
a seeker of souls. He should not be one who just stood on
the door-step. He was to get into the house, win a welcome
by the fireside, have time for a cup of tea, a word in season
and, more often than not, a prayer. He must not be,
declared William Booth, a man merely after money but a
family counsellor, a pastoral visitor, a representative of

God.   To William Booth this family-counselling, home-
visiting agent was the chief justification for the Army's
entering life assurance at all.   The thousands of week-by-
week collectors were to be Salvationists who would take the
Army's message, the Army's uniform, with consecrated
ability to advise and give practical aid on a hundred and one
problems.   It could never be just a matter of money.

The argument of those who opposed the foundation of
the Society, including George Scott Railton, was that it was
' commercialization '.   Time was to show that this was not a
correct description.   William and Bramwell Booth, Carleton
and the rest were right.   The history of The Salvation Army
Assurance Society reveals a society which could render a
magnificent spiritual and social service while still operating
as an efficient life office.

This holds good, even in these days of affluence.   It may
be true that working-class families have incomes of £20 to
£30 or more a week but they spend it quickly and often
spend up to the full amount of their income every week.
Some spend more.   Hire-purchase agreements and financial
commitments on the car and the holidays soak up the money
before its recipients realize it.   In some cases, smoking,
drinking and gambling divert wages from proper objects,
so that relatively good pay does not enable some workers to
avoid debts, leave alone save money.

So, for one reason or another, there is a large segment
of the population that prefers the regular weekly call of the
Salvation Army Assurance Society agent or the agent of
some other society.   Working-class parents who have
endowment policies on their children, or an endowment
retirement policy on the wage-earner, find that saving is
fostered and the quite considerable premium safely passed
over because the Army agent calls at a certain time on a
certain day.   He has become a family habit as well as a friend.
The extent of such savings can be indicated by the assurance
Table 17B, under which, for a weekly premium of 10s., a
thirty-year-old policy-holder secures £1,000 at the age of
sixty-five or at previous death.   On Salvation Army Assurance

Society tables, bonuses on industrial branch policies total 15 per cent at ten years, and 30 per cent at twenty-five years, all of which shows the industrial branch policy to be not so ' old-fashioned ' as some critics would assert. There is no gainsaying that millions of policy-holders, affluence notwithstanding, prefer it before all others.

It is a happy thought that the Booths, father and son, with Bremner, Carleton and the rest, who thought of The Salvation Army Assurance Society as a soul-saving, salvation soldier-making force—in addition to raising funds for the war—could look at it now, so many years afterwards, and find that its basic aims and methods are their own.

The following pages give details of present-day agents of the Society, those dual-purpose ' ordinands ' of William Booth, who in these latter days function as assurance society men and soul-seeking Salvationists at one and the same time.

A Large Amount of Money

A Field Department assessment of Agent Sam. W. Weaver, of Thornton Heath:

> *He has been with the Society since 1930. He was recently called to Chief Office by the Managing Director for the purpose of receiving a presentation in recognition of his prowess as an ordinary branch canvasser. This won for him the position of Ordinary Branch Champion for the Society for 1963, 1964, and 1965. An ardent Salvationist at all times, Agent Weaver was always to be seen on Society work in full Salvation Army uniform.*

He became interested in The Salvation Army Assurance Society when a visiting officer suggested he should leave his job as an engineer and become an agent. He pointed out that Sam could earn a large amount of money! A more convincing argument was that there would be ample opportunity for evangelistic work. Let Agent Weaver continue in his own words:

' The going was hard and the people not very kindly disposed toward The Salvation Army Assurance Society, and so, after a few weeks, with no fortune made, not making enough to pay for my lodgings, I decided to quit. But I was advised by a friend to give it one more try, to get out on the knocker and canvass a little. I did feel that God was leading me to work he wanted me to do, so I persevered.

'After searching for a very small road, with as few houses as possible, I started door-knocking. What an experience—practically every door was slammed in my face! I decided to finish the one side of the street and if it produced no results then I would take it that I was not cut out for assurance work.

' Still the results did not come, and so, very disappointed I left the street and had a look round the shops.

' I had a feeling of crisis and could not escape the feeling that God was working in my life. Someone seemed to say to me, " Go back! Go back! "

'After a lot of heart-searching and hesitation I went back. The first door I knocked at was opened by an old lady who said: " Thank God, you have come! I saw you across the road and hoped you would. Could you help me? I am all alone. My husband is in the front room, dying. Will you pray with him, before he dies? "

' I went in. The old man seemed too far gone to understand as I read from the Scriptures. I knelt down and prayed, wondering if any good could come out of it.

' Later that night I went back and remained all night. In the early hours of the morning the old man opened his eyes.

' " Would you be the young man who prayed with me yesterday? " he said.

' " Yes," said I.

' " Then would you do it all over again," replied the man. I read to him John 3: 16 and parts of John 14. I spoke to him of heaven. As I prayed he found Christ. He told me so.

' I felt then, and feel today, so many years after, that God led me to that door and showed me the work I was to do for Him. The news went around the town. I began to feel confident both as an Army assurance agent and as an evangelist. The Salvation Army had already established itself and was respected by the people. God was working through The Salvation Army Assurance Society.

' People often say you cannot mix business with religion, but after nearly thirty-seven years as an agent I must contradict this opinion.

' I had been calling at a home for some years. The housewife was a bad client and I had tried to get her off my book because of her heavy arrears. She was hardly ever free of black eyes and bruises inflicted by her husband.

' One day she said to me, " I wish I was like you; you always seem happy when you call here each week."

' I must confess I was most anxious to get away from the house. It was not a place that invited long acquaintance. But she returned to the subject and this time I told her she could be happy, that Christ could change her life completely. Later she asked me to tell her more. This time I had to enter the home.

' There was no place to put one's hat; the table looked as if it had not been cleared for months; a newspaper was the " table-cloth "; the floor had not been swept for a long, long time. But even though I had hesitated God was in that home that day.

' I told the woman to pray for herself.

' She replied, " God knows you better than me. Will you tell Him about me and see if He can help me ? "

' Kneeling on that dirty floor, I prayed with this poor woman though, I am ashamed to confess, my faith remained low.

'A fortnight later I called late one evening, and the door was opened by a well-built man, the husband, I presumed, the blacker of eyes and bestower of bruises. His opening remark scared me—" What the hell have you been doing to my old woman ? "

' I kept calm and remained in one piece and he went on:

" She got religion! The place has been cleaned up. She cooks good meals. She is a different woman! "

' This great news cheered me up.

' " Sir," I said, " it is not me, but God. I told her about Him."

' Some time later I learned that husband and wife had joined a mission and the home was transformed. Now all that began as a business call. Business and religion *do* work side by side.

'Another woman would look from behind the curtains when I called and often would not open the door.

' One day I saw her leaving a public house, a few doors from her home, and she informed me that she had looked in to see the time!

' Evidently her clock was a poor timekeeper because I often found her there and the time came when it was necessary for me to call at the pub to collect her assurance premiums.

' But sometimes I was allowed indoors and would have a chat with the woman and her husband, and I discovered that the woman had been a Christian until she found that " beer is best ".

' By the blessing of God I had the joy of introducing the woman to the Army. She was converted and became a good soldier.

' For me, as for many other Salvation Army Assurance Society agents, my work has entailed much more than the collection of premiums. It has meant watching all night with people who were dying, visiting the sick, praying with folk in their homes, helping to repair broken marriages, giving advice and help when girls go wrong, arranging funerals for women who had no one to turn to in their trouble.

' Of course, sometimes there has been wry humour. One night I was asked if I could do a person a great kindness. Not knowing what this was, but willing to be of help, I replied recklessly that I would only be too pleased.

' It transpired that the woman had just lost her husband.

" I would be obliged if you will shave him and make him look nice and clean," she said.

' I was taken up to the bedroom where the dead man lay alone. The room was dimly lit by candles. I was left alone to my grim task. And as I worked striving hard to keep my hand from trembling, shadows cast weird shapes, dancing on the walls, as the draught made the candles flicker. I doubt whether the deceased ever had a quicker shave! The experience gave me confidence and I have shaved several dead men since.

' Some of this was years ago but I am still welcome in the homes of the people. A few months ago I canvassed a road in South Norwood and discovered that almost all the householders were coloured immigrants. But I was invited into their homes and told of their problems. They assumed that as a Salvationist I was a man who could help. They told me the amount of rent they paid, the length of time they had been in the country, the kind of work they did. Several have become policy-holders of the Society.

' When I call on Saturday afternoons the children are waiting at the windows for the Army man to call. What a welcome I get! A chair is pulled up and the West Indians crowd round. Then I must forget the time for a little while, and I listen to the family news. Such is their confidence in their new friend.

' I feel that William Booth would be most pleased at this aspect of the work of the Society he founded, for numbers of people have been converted, just because his agents call at the homes of the people " and mix religion with business ".'

The Best Job in the Army

A Field Department assessment:

Agent O. J. Wells, of Blackburn, recently received the Civic Medal as a mark of the town council's appreciation of his years of service not only in The Salvation Army but for the community. He has been an agent since 1913 and found it a highly satisfying task. He regards himself as an assurance agent-plus, and accepts with great joy the many opportunities that have come his way to mix business with religion. He helps the people in their homes, knowing himself to be an ambassador for Christ as he goes from house to house.

He tells his own story:

' For me it all began when I was serving my time at engineering, at Barrow-in-Furness. The sister of the corps officer came over for a holiday from Bolton, Lancashire. A romance began. I was a young bandsman. I soon realized that if I wanted to see my young lady as often as I wished then I must get work nearer her home. I moved in 1913 and was soon playing in the Army band at Blackburn. But I was out of work.

'After a Sunday's meetings a Captain Hodgson and Adjutant Whitehead spoke to me regarding an agency with The Salvation Army Assurance Society. After some thought I decided to take on a debit of £5, which would bring me in about 19s. a week. Now is my chance, I thought. I wanted to do good and if I became an agent I knew I would have the opportunity to which God was calling me—visiting the homes of the people, the sick and bereaved, helping those with domestic problems. I soon found that I had the best job in the Army! What a privilege! And this door to service was open to me for the next forty-two years.

'As an agent I held my own most years and on two or three occasions was top in the North-West Division for ordinary branch. In industrial branch I had an increase for most of the forty-two years. While I served in H.M. Forces in India, my wife, who had been a real helpmate to me, kept the business going for three years. I would have been nothing without her.

' Service as a local officer has included forty-three years as Corps Treasurer. I am still the Treasurer. I still play in the band, my commission being dated 1907.

' Perhaps the most satisfying and blessed part of an agent's life is when people come for advice about their children and other domestic problems. Not only has it been my joy to influence people to attend the Army, but by the grace of God it has been my privilege to help to solve family disputes, even bringing about the reconciliation of man and wife.

'There is no doubt in my mind that an agent in our Society has a good appointment if he regards it as a calling and not just a job.

'During the Army's Centenary Year the town council of Blackburn, feeling that it should express its appreciation for the Army locally, decided to award me the Civic Medal as a mark of honour for all the years of service to the Army and to the community.* At the meeting of presentation there were over two thousand people present. To God be all the glory!'

Gruel for the Baby

Agent Harry Martin, of Harlesden, now retired, proves that there are always exceptions to rules—he was never a canvasser, yet his 'book' grew enormously—'natural growth' he called it!

The secret, as with so many other Salvation Army Assurance Society agents, was his character and pleasing personality. He was a naturally good 'mixer', quite without shyness, able to talk on any subject when there was need to set his clients at ease. He was often something of a travelling 'citizens' advice bureau', sharply intelligent, not narrow-minded, certainly not 'pious', in the off-putting sense of that word, yet every inch a good Salvationist. Of course, he worked hard. How else could he chalk up a £50 net increase in five years? In forty years as an agent he never had a disputed claim and usually it was his boast that no other agent of any other society could pay a claim quicker than he could.

Yet Harry took The Salvation Army Assurance Society job without enthusiasm—he had married the daughter of a

*A woman officer was similarly honoured on the same occasion— Major Alice Peel (R.).

Salvation Army Assurance Society Divisional Manager who had persuaded him that an agency was to be preferred to life in a customs and excise warehouse. Harry had his doubts at first, although he soon found there was more to the Salvation Army job than collecting shillings and pence.

He remembers calling at a home where a sick woman was unable to make gruel for her baby's breakfast. So Harry made it, and a cup of tea for the distressed mother as well.

He was often asked to pray for the sick and became the only link many people had with religion. To them Harry Martin, the cheerful assurance agent, was The Salvation Army. Though he made a good financial living this was never the main consideration. He prospered, winning Salvation Army Assurance Society awards for outstanding increases on more than one occasion, yet success never spoiled him. When he had a car, a bank balance, a house, or even two, he remained the same unspoiled man and energetic and loyal Salvationist. In retirement now, somewhere on the Kent coast, he thanks God for a happy life, a good wife, two Salvationist children, a few grandchildren and not least the memories of a task well done. William Booth, Bramwell, Carleton and others might be somewhat astonished at this sort of affluent Salvationism. But it had to come; today it is commonplace and in many cases, as in Harry Martin's, it can stand up to the most searching scrutiny—even the Franciscan Railton need not be ashamed of it!

He Wanted Ice-cream

The Field Department's assessment of Agent Miss D. Draper, of Liverpool:

In addition to successfully negotiating her duties as a Salvation Army Assurance Society agent, she finds time to give satisfactory service not only as a Salvationist, but also as a splendid local officer in her corps.

She tells her own story:

' I served for some time as a goodwill officer and have always endeavoured to weave the spirit of that service into my work as an Army assurance agent. I learned to love people, realizing that in the many hundreds of homes I would visit would be the challenge for me to give such as I have. The door of service as an agent is a wonderful opportunity. Behind the smiling face of the person who opens the door there is often a heavy heart. While in the house, signing the premium receipt book or having a little chat, many confidences, sorrows and joys have been expressed. The book of names of clients given to me when I began as an agent has now become a list of people with needs, families with problems. And so my prayer, each day, as I set out on my journey, is—" Constancy to me impart; stablish with Thy grace my heart ". Many of my policy-holders have become my friends. There await me in the homes of the people many more cups of tea or coffee than I can drink, but more than that, much more.

' Over a quick " cuppa " not only is business booked up but spiritual need is revealed. With God's help, " Such as I have I give ", the word in season, the prayer at the table, together, especially in the hour of bereavement. Then hearts are tender, mellowed by grief. What a privilege is mine to bring words of comfort, a prayer of consolation, not of the grave, but of the certainty of the Resurrection!

' From my experience I would say that the Salvation Army Assurance Society agent is one of the most welcomed into the homes of the people of all types, creeds and nationalities. Palatial homes, shops, middle-class homes, and also the hovels where people seem content to exist in squalor, are visited.

' There is a humorous side. One lady I found anxiously waiting for my call one Monday morning. She wanted to take out a new policy. " What a good start ", I thought to myself, " for Monday morning, and without canvassing." So I brought out my prospectus and proposal cards and asked her what type of policy she needed.

E—A.U.S.

' " Oh," she said, " I want 2s. or 2s. 6d. on my husband —the doctor told him yesterday that he had thrombosis! "

'Although my disappointment at losing my Monday morning new business was keen, I saw the comical side and advised the lady that no business could be booked on the life of her husband. She was, however, determined to take out another policy so she booked another 2s. on her own life.

' Late one Friday evening, among my last calls, was a woman whose father had just been discharged from hospital as incurable. I entered the room where the old man was weeping. He wanted ice-cream! Nothing else would satisfy him so, at 9.45 p.m., I set off to try to find a shop where the old man's craving could be satisfied. I found a woman locking up the premises, but on hearing my story she reopened for a moment or two to supply me with a family block of ice-cream. I delivered this to the old gentleman.

' When next I called the daughter informed me that her father had passed away. " Your ice-cream was the one thing he enjoyed most of all before he went," she said.

' On the following Friday when I called for the premium money, she asked me in and stood holding a little casket. She opened it to show me the contents.

' " These are Dad's ashes. I'm going to scatter them about the cemetery! "

'As an assurance agent-plus, I am deeply conscious that all matters of business must be dealt with in the spirit of the great theme of the Society, " Holiness unto the Lord ". The standard of Salvationism must be held high—for people respect and honour the name of The Salvation Army and all it stands for.

'At the Christmas season of goodwill I always pick out six or seven old people, or chronically sick people, whom I call upon with parcels of groceries. This is part of my Christian stewardship. Sometimes a policy-holder will ask me if I can accept a parcel of clothes that her family has outgrown, or a three-piece suite she is replacing with a contemporary one. Then I remember needy policy-holders who will appreciate such gifts.

' Sometimes I find dire poverty. I went to see one family late at night, and asked if they would accept some really good beds, complete with interior sprung mattresses, pillows, blankets and the rest. The children exclaimed: " Oh, now we shall have a real bed! "

' What visitation the Salvation Army Assurance Society agent does in the course of a week! What a multitude of homes visited! Business, Christian witness and friendship are all mixed in a valuable and helpful relationship.'

Contact Man

Field Department details:

Agent Leonard Hutchinson, of Londonderry, Northern Ireland, was appointed agent of the Society in 1931. He has been outstandingly successful and through his work gained wide influence in civic affairs. Recently he was elected a City Councillor for Londonderry and has served on various committees, on the Citizens' Advice Bureau, on the North-West Council of Social Services, and also the local Education Committee. Both with the individual policy-holder and with the community at large, he is held in the highest regard.

The man who collects the Salvation Army Assurance Society premiums in Londonderry takes pride in the walled city, famous for the siege of 1688, and for the hymns which have girdled the globe from the pen of Mrs. Alexander, wife of a Bishop of Derry and Raphoe. These include, ' There is a green hill far away ' and ' Once in royal David's city '. Agent Hutchinson adds that ' He pardoned a rebel ' also found its birthplace in Londonderry.

He claims that, though farthest away from the Chief Office, Londonderry is truest to its heart. Commissioners Carleton and McAlonan, key figures in the development of the Society, were born eighty miles away, near Belfast. Agent Hutchinson was born and dedicated as a child in Londonderry and his name is now synonymous with The

Salvation Army and its Assurance Society. In thirty-five years Leonard Hutchinson broke every record in the book, including the supreme championship (still unbeaten), ordinary branch for 1943, and the industrial branch for 1963.

As he had completed his apprenticeship as an engineer, Hutchinson was greatly opposed by his Salvationist parents when he decided to become an agent in The Salvation Army Assurance Society. They expected him to do better in life. Some agents were so shabby that they were referred to as the 'down-at-heel brigade'. But his parents lived to rejoice in his success. Announcing his election to the City Corporation, a newspaper referred to him as 'an official of The Salvation Army Assurance Society'; then went on, 'Perhaps no member of Londonderry Corporation has appeared on so many platforms, acting as speaker, chairman and artist. In his younger days he was a noted cornet soloist.'

His wife, formerly Woman Head Constable of the Royal Ulster Constabulary, is also on the Marriage Guidance Council.

If asked about his success Hutchinson may point to the fly-leaf of his collecting book, where he has written a sentence from Proverbs—'A word fitly spoken is like apples of gold in pictures of silver'. In an earlier collecting book he had inscribed, 'It all depends on me, and I depend on God'.

He finds no conflict between the commercial side and the religious side of his work. On the contrary, one often opens the door to the other. He is accepted in the homes of the people not only as a business man but as a spiritual adviser. With the falling away of churchgoing this aspect of his work becomes more and more important. The agent as a 'home missionary', the Founder's idea, is more than ever effective.

If The Salvation Army Assurance Society merely paid its way, with no profit at all, Hutchinson believes it would still be a worth while evangelistic, social and pastoral enterprise. The Founder is taken at his word when he lays down the twofold objective of the agent: ' Striving to get people to insure their lives *and* their soul's salvation.'

Agent Hutchinson recalls saying frankly to a publican, ' I bring life and hope and protection to the people; you bring misery and anguish! ' It was a hard saying, at which many a man would have been offended, but the publican was so dismayed and conscience-stricken that he closed his pub, bought a grocery business and now takes communion regularly!

Hutchinson insists that life assurance, as he conducts it, matches the motto of the Society: 'Holiness unto the Lord', and salvation, too.

The agent, the 'Booth missionary', brings the Army and its message to hundreds of people who, otherwise, would know nothing about it. He does not seek to evade the practical and even mundane implications of such good-will. Many people on his books have remembered the Army in their wills, some of them having never heard an Army band, or read *The War Cry*. Their sole liaison with The Salvation Army had been Agent Hutchinson. He called on one man for twenty-five years, not realizing that any impression had been made, then learned that the man had left £2,000 to the Army. Sometimes the agent has introduced one of his clients to the corps officer. It has proved a highly profitable meeting—for the client.

Of course he admits that it is the name ' Salvation Army ' which is the open sesame to so many doors and hearts. He seeks always to remember that as the representative of the Army much is expected of him—the highest standards of spiritual life.

On the professional side, thinking of the science of life assurance, Agent Hutchinson has faced the problem of changing social patterns. His clients include the professional classes, doctors, ministers of religion, veterinary surgeons, architects, university professors, farmers, engineers, sur-veyors and many others. Obviously such men prefer ordinary branch assurance. But this Ulsterman sells his middle-class clients industrial branch policies!

He has the largest agency in the Society and part of the reason for this achievement, he insists, is that he has been able to place policies of both ordinary branch and industrial branch category with professional people. There are few 'working-class' people on his books—and one wonders what William Booth would think of that!

Making a Name for Himself

Streets, squares and mountains have been named after the illustrious, but one Salvation Army assurance agent, who would consider himself not at all illustrious, has given his name to a block of flats—the *John Lester Court*, at Salford, Lancashire.

The Salford Reporter commented: 'This is a name not likely to be treated with the indifference usually felt toward a building block, for it is named after "Johnnie" Lester, quiet and unassuming ex-Mayor and council veteran. For fifty years he lived in St. Paul's Ward; for thirty years he represented it on the Council; for thirty-seven years he has been winning friends in the area as agent for The Salvation Army. He is as well known for his Christian witness as a Salvationist and Army assurance representative, as for his many years' association with the Salford Council. As an Alderman, Agent Lester served on six committees, having been chairman of one for eighteen years. He was Mayor of Salford in 1954 and again in 1955.'

Even more to the point, the newspaper assessment is confirmed by the many thousands of clients on whom Agent Lester has called in the course of his work. Civic duties were never second to Christ's service—although, of course, there is a sense in which they are one and the same—but Mayor Lester or Councillor Lester never took precedence over 'the insurance man', who was a welcome visitor, a friend of the family, an ambassador for Christ. Like many another who combines the business of life assurance with work for God, Agent Lester's name is written large on the fields of labour where he has served his

Master, written indeed on the lives of those he has coun-
selled in God's name. To him this is greater than seeing
his name blazoned on John Lester Court.

Not Just an Agent

*Agent J. Ivor Parsell, of Shawlands, Glasgow, has
represented the Society continuously since March, 1925, and,
although already past the age for retirement, is still engaged
in a full-time capacity on agency work. He has received various
Society awards for progress made, and was chosen by his
colleagues to be Chairman of the Association of Agents of The
Salvation Army Assurance Society Limited. He has also been
an outstanding example of Salvationism in his corps at Govan.*

He tells his own story:

' I was a shipwright on Clydeside, in 1925, when I
applied for an agency with The Salvation Army Assurance
Society. Shipyards were very slack at this time. I was
appointed to a Glasgow agency and soon realized that I was
not just an agent, but that I was entering houses as a
Salvationist and representative of the Lord Jesus Christ.
I have striven by God's blessing to live up to this high
calling.

' Of course the commercial side of assurance can be
reconciled with the religious side. Our Founder would not
have taken the Society if he had not been sure on this point.
Assurance is an honest contract, genuinely helpful to the
policy-holder.

' There has been no conflict between business and religion as far as I am concerned. Some good people have
questioned me as to why the Army should have an Assurance Society and I have explained the Founder's idea—
Salvationists visiting so many homes, and being a real
help in time of need, not only with assurance benefits but
the assurance of God's love. This still stands today.

' Time and time again I get the chance to declare my
faith and give my testimony. I have been asked to pray in
sickness and death. I have also prayed without being asked.

I do as I feel led to do. This applies to Roman Catholic clients as well as others. Sometimes I have been asked to conduct the funeral. On one occasion I was asked to officiate and say grace at a golden wedding anniversary celebration. I have been in this one district for over thirty-four years. People confide in me because I represent the Army and, I hope, because I am a true and worthy representative of the Kingdom of God.

' Young people today do not just accept me because I am a Salvationist. They question my belief and ask questions. This I find is a great responsibility and opportunity.'

Influence More than Affluence

Agent Albert Punton, of Belmont, Durham. Appointed agent in the Society, January 1939, *and was Bandmaster at Sherburn Hill Corps from* 1955 *to* 1966.

He is financially one of the most successful agents of the Society, but he regards influence as a Christian as more important than affluence. For some years he has been Secretary of the Association of Agents of The Salvation Army Assurance Society Limited and in that position has done much to maintain goodwill between the staff and management.

He tells his own story:

' I have been with the Society for over twenty-seven years and found it an interesting and, at times, an exciting experience. When I began I found myself collecting approximately £10 per week. In those days this proved to be hard work. Now, with increased debit both in the industrial branch and the ordinary branch, I find I am collecting about £10,000 a year. Nevertheless, the sound basic training I had in my early days stands me in good stead.

' There have been many challenging situations—I find that the Salvation Army Assurance Society agent must be a man of many parts. Perhaps this is why I have remained with the Society although there have been tempting offers to work for other companies. The fact is that as a Salvationist one is more than an agent. I have always found happiness in the thought that I am able to serve God as well as the people in the course of my daily work.

'For some years I have served as General Secretary of The Association of Agents of The Salvation Army Assurance Society Limited. We have discussion with the management at least twice yearly and I have found this has been the means of cementing relationships between the management and the agents. Today our relationship is of the highest order. In my own career tribute must be paid to my wife, who at all times has given me her valuable support. Without her I could not have achieved half of what I have done.

'I came to the agency from the Sherburn Hill colliery. I had often wanted to escape from coal mining and though I knew little or nothing about assurance, after hard training and study I found that I was able to grasp the essentials of the work. Ever since, with the exception of the war years, when I was in the Forces, I have put my heart and soul into the job. I am firmly convinced that the work was a calling given me by God and to Him I give praise.

'I am asked if I have found that the commercial side can be reconciled with the religious side. As far as I am concerned I do not think the two can be divorced. I have never at any time felt there has been conflict one with the other.

'Among my clients ten per cent are Salvationists and the others a cross-section of the general public. Practically every religious denomination is represented on my book, many of my policy-holders being Roman Catholics. From the latter my Salvationism and religious convictions receive the greatest respect. It can be said that all clients are happy to feel that as they do themselves a service by taking out life assurance they are also benefiting a worth-while cause, The Salvation Army.

'As with other agents, I find that because of my Salvationism I am often called upon to render spiritual aid in times of need. People expect from me that little extra, the word in season, the prayer, the " God bless you ". This is where the Army agent is unique. Our uniform and our faith introduces that extra and highly important factor—

religion. At one home, as I leave, I always say " God bless you." The woman with whom I leave this greeting once told me, " You will never know what those words mean to me." Even if my ministry were this alone I would feel that God is using me. Not the least of the joys of my work is that of calling at the homes of people who share with me the week-end meetings at the Army. Also, on Monday morning, the blessings are renewed as we talk of God's goodness.

' During my lifetime as an agent I have striven to keep first things first and God has helped me in many ways. It has been hard at times to go into people's homes and discuss their religious beliefs. For me, talking about religion does not come easily. But always I am cheered by the thought: I can show them what God has done for me. My life must be an example.

' Of course, it is not always the spoken word that means the most. Recently a client said to me—a man whose knowledge did not come from any words of mine—" If ever I need spiritual help, Mr. Punton, I have told my wife to call on you." He was thinking of serious illness, bereavement, his own death even. There were ministers to whom he might have turned but he wanted the Army agent. It was a compliment indeed and I give God the glory. Of course, I have often invited people to the Army and from such invitations two families at least have been won for God. Whether in uniform or out of it I am known as " the Army man ", and I never forget that the kindness and respect that I receive, the opportunities for service that constantly arise, are because of the Army and the Kingdom of God.

' There is danger for the man who forgets why he was placed on so high a pedestal by the people. As I am welcomed into their homes I pray that God will be with me and that He shall have the glory.

'After all these years, going through the doors of the houses is just like going home. There is a feeling of understanding between my clients and myself that cannot be explained in terms of premiums and assurance coverage.

' I celebrated twenty-five years with the Society about three years ago, at a festival to mark the occasion. The Army hall was packed to capacity. Extra seating had to be brought in and many people were turned away. It was a deeply moving experience and I took it as a sign that God had honoured my work down through the years.'

She Left Him Holding the Baby

Agent W. D. Rowlands, of Porth, Glamorgan, has served the Society since 1936, with an intermission in H.M. Forces during the Second World War. For this he was awarded the M.B.E. He still holds the military rank of Major.

He tells his own story:

'After leaving the Welsh Guards, between the wars, I returned to Porth, where I was born. I was married with one child. My wife belonged to a well-known Salvationist family and had been a Salvationist all her life.

' South Wales, and particularly the Rhondda, was in the grip of the great industrial depression of the thirties, "the slump". I found myself one of the great army of unemployed, and remained in this state for about eighteen months, until I obtained work as a labourer, helping to take up tram tracks when the Rhondda Transport Company introduced a bus service. I was a bandsman, and still am, at Porth Corps.

' They were trying days, dark days, but days when we proved over and over again that God does certainly answer prayer.

' On the completion of this work I was again unemployed for a few months when, " out of the blue ", as it seemed, Lieut.-Colonel Frederick Warren, who was the Divisional Manager for the Cardiff area, asked me if I would become an agent for the Society. If I accepted it meant that I must move from Porth to Bargoed. I prayed much about this matter. We had little money and at this time my wife had to undergo a serious operation at the Cardiff Royal Infirmary. She remained there for nearly three months.

'Nevertheless, God showed us the way! On March 13, 1936, I was appointed to the Bargoed Agency. This move took me into the home of Mrs. Percy Butland, a widow, whose husband had been the agent for Bargoed. Mrs. Buckland, a quiet unassuming person, was a devout Christian who helped me a great deal, not only with agency affairs but in spiritual matters also. (She has since been promoted to Glory, but her influence lives on in her son, who is Captain Howard Butland, of the British Territory.)

'Always I have tried to remember that I am first a Christian and secondly a Salvationist assurance agent. During the whole of my service I have never been involved in a business transaction where my Christian faith and my life assurance occupation could not be reconciled. Indeed, I have found that because of my Christian principles people have confidence in the Army where the business details of assurance are concerned. Without making any boast, giving God the glory, I can claim to have gained the respect and confidence of the people I have dealt with, because in my work I have sincerely tried to carry out the teachings of the Lord Jesus Christ.

'Of course, when one is dealing with people day by day, as we do in assurance work, there are bound to be happenings apart from the business side. It has always been my practice to pray with people in their homes when family troubles have come. Most of the people have certainly appreciated such prayer.

'A few years ago I had to ask a woman client, firmly but politely, to reduce the arrears on the policies she held. Perhaps I was *too firm*. Anyhow, on my next visit to her home her husband was waiting for me! He threatened to hit me, and goodness knows what! I listened, wondering how I was to emerge from this perilous situation. After he had cooled down a little I told the irate husband that if he so desired he could hit me. But first I would ask him to allow me to pray with him. He was so astonished at this that he became more or less speechless. I prayed with him and his wife; he did not hit me. Although he made no profession of Christianity the Army was always welcomed at his home from that time forward. When he died recently it was found that he had requested that the Army should conduct his funeral. I believe he sought Christ before he died.

' Once, when I was collecting, a young woman on whom I called asked me to watch the baby for a few moments while she went to a shop, a few yards down the street. I agreed, but she did not come back, and I was left holding the baby, figuratively and literally. It transpired that she was running away from her husband, who had not treated her well. But as I knew both the families, by the blessing of God and prayer and patience the Army was able to bring husband and wife together again.

'I find I am more than ever welcome in people's homes because now I am doing business with the third and even the fourth generation.

' During the Second World War I had a break of five and a half years. I became a Major in command of a unit, I was mentioned in dispatches three times and finally was awarded the M.B.E. for services following D-day in Normandy.

'Although I received attractive offers of other jobs, I went back to The Salvation Army Assurance Society.

' God has been good to my family and to me over the years. It is my prayer that I may continue to serve Him as long as He wills as an agent in The Salvation Army Assurance Society.'

INVESTMENT POLICY
AND FIRE INSURANCE

THOUGH The Salvation Army Assurance Society came into existence in 1891 it commemorated seventy years' of life assurance in 1964, for it had been in existence three years before the first life policy was issued. At the public celebrations, led by the Chief of the Staff at Clapton Congress Hall in March, 1964, the Chief revealed that in the seventy years annual premium income had grown from £420 in 1894 to £3,000,000 in 1963.

The Managing Director, in a seventieth-year comment on the Society's finances, pointed out that the valuation surplus was £1,120,919 at the end of 1963. A bonus of £2 10s. 0d. per cent of the sum assured was declared on all ordinary branch policies entitled to profit and the Society made large allocations from surpluses to industrial branch policy-holders also.

The Commissioner reminded his readers that, in 1900, a financial newspaper had prophesied of the Society: 'It is going to be a big thing.' But long before 1964 it was quite clear that The Salvation Army Assurance Society would never compete with the giants in point of size. Rather, its role would be, 'Not the biggest, but one of the best', as the Managing Director put it.

The year 1964 saw the annual income from investments top the million mark. Investments, or rather interest from them, make up the true riches of any assurance society. They represent skilled, long-term effort, the accumulation of pennies, shillings and pounds by devoted pioneers and present-day workers, like the slow, sure growth of an oak tree, which requires fifty years before its stature and strength as a tree can be seen and appreciated. In any well-established society regular premiums will pay claims and expenses but only a large and well-conducted investment policy will make profits, without which, in these days no life office could survive.

Investment policy is a special concern of Mr. Cecil J. Matthews who joined the Society in 1911, and has therefore served under every Managing Director from Carleton to the present day. In 1930 he went to the Investments Department, serving under Colonel Railton Howard of whom he holds the highest opinion. The Colonel's grasp of investment matters was expert, and Mr. Matthews admits that all he had to do was develop the policy so skilfully initiated. In particular this development has included investment of insurance funds in the Stock Exchange share market. Previously investments had been almost exclusively in Government stocks and fixed interest guaranteed securities.

The Army's religious and ethical standards pose a problem for anyone responsible for investing the Society's funds. In the age of take-overs and mergers the ' respectable ' company of today is the pariah of tomorrow. Recently the Army found that its shares in a highly reputable group of companies had been ' tainted ' by that company's acquisition of a wine and spirits subsidiary. It is Mr. Matthews's duty, in line with the policy of The Salvation Army Assurance Society Investment Council, to dispose of such shares as quickly as possible even if, as is the case sometimes, this occasions a loss of capital.

Such a transaction may rest upon a seemingly trifling detail, as was the case when one big group concerned in dairy products merged with another of the same sort. The latter company owned but one licensed bar yet, because of this, the Society sold its highly profitable holdings in the group. It was the price to be paid for a principle.

Mr. Matthews and his staff have to be alert to the regroupings and wide ramifications of six to seven hundred companies to ensure that the investment policy of The Salvation Army Assurance Society can withstand the most meticulous scrutiny on moral and religious grounds.

The amount of money dealt with by the Society's investment office can seem astronomically large although The

Salvation Army Assurance Society is small by comparison with some other life offices. At the end of 1967 a gross sum of over £27,000,000 was invested in Stock Exchange shares, fixed interest securities, property, and so on.

Almost certainly the average policy-holder has no idea how important the Society's investments are to him. A policy-holder nowadays expects profit even on an industrial branch policy. Indeed, in The Salvation Army Assurance Society industrial branch the return of profit allocated to policy-holders is about half a million yearly.

In its contact with the stock market the Society has the services of brokers, who have been associated with the Army for many years. Investment transactions of the sort required necessitate speedy action, for in the business world today there is more money to invest than there are good shares to buy. Yet it goes without saying that although promptitude is essential, caution is also necessary

Experience and skill of a very high order are essential if these two seemingly contradictory qualities are to be combined.

The successful insurance investor is constantly seeking to secure the most attractive return and security for the funds made available. Loan capital maturing in, say, seventy years at current rates of say $7\frac{1}{2}$ per cent per annum is most attractive. As existing holdings approach redemption date every effort must be made to reinvest and so extend the life of the loan. This is of special importance when interest rates are high.

As a holder of share capital the Society becomes part owner of many companies and participates in their development and growth. Income derived from this class of investment fluctuates in accordance with the success of the enterprise, but with careful selection it can be very rewarding. To the uninitiated it seems like easy money: an annual return to The Salvation Army Assurance Society of about one and a half million pounds every year, in investment income alone. But it must be remembered that by far the larger part of this sum belongs to the policy-holders who number many thousands.

One thing is certain—the cynics, who nourish the myth that all connections with the ' City ' are suspect, that stocks and shares are a species of gambling, that brokers and investment experts are Dickensian style ' get rich quick merchants ', are far from the truth.   Cecil J. Matthews is a Salvationist, like many another in his field, a man of the highest Christian probity.   Walking into his small but efficient department one finds a Salvationist staff, and the ' climate' is that which one would find in any other area of Salvation Army activity where the highest concern for spiritual standards is emphasized.

One can be sure that when the policy of the Society is considered at the Investment Council—of which the Army's Chancellor of the Exchequer and the Managing Director of The Salvation Army Assurance Society are members—then Cecil J. Matthews, who is the executive officer, puts first things first.

THE SALVATION ARMY FIRE INSURANCE CORPORATION LIMITED, with its present headquarters at 4 Holywell Hill, St. Albans, Herts., began as the Fire Insurance Department of International Headquarters.   Like The Salvation Army Assurance Society it was born of a Salvationist need—the necessity for ' cover ' for the ever-increasing number of Army properties.   The many forms of fire insurance hitherto existing had become complicated as well as expensive, and when an alarming fire occurred at International Headquarters the Founder and his advisers determined in future to arrange their own insurance.

In 1890, as the result of an advertisement in *The War Cry*, David Wales of Scotland left his job as a fire assessor's assistant to become the foundation member of the Fire Insurance Department.   At first the policy was to arrange cover for all Salvation Army buildings and be content with that.   The first Fire Insurance circular was printed in 1899 and quoted Oliver Cromwell: ' Trust in God and keep your powder dry.'   Cover to the amount of £50 was offered for a premium of 1s. 3d.

But in 1900 the Fire Insurance Department was transferred to Commissioner Carleton's administration in The Salvation Army Assurance Society. It was not until 1909 that the present Salvation Army Fire Insurance Corporation Limited was registered at the Board of Trade. At its first directors' meeting, February 26, 1909, Bramwell Booth was in the chair with such well-known men as Higgins, Simpson, Hurren and the omnipresent Carleton in support. Lieut.-Colonel George Mitchell was the first Managing Director and Major William F. Giles the first Secretary. The Corporation joined the National Fire Offices Committee, and the salvage authorities of London and Glasgow, in 1913.

Policies are now issued to the general public and the range has been extended to burglary, plate-glass and motor insurance; in fact, all insurance other than life. Lieut.-Colonel Arthur P. Tilney, the present Secretary/Manager, kindly supplied the data from which this brief summary is drawn.

›

Chapter Twenty-six

STAFF WELFARE ASSOCIATIONS

WITH the passing of the years staff welfare, and particularly the relationships of management with employees, became of ever-increasing importance. William Booth, Carleton, and the rest knew little of industrial psychology, although their instinct for developing a good *modus operandi* between men and management was normally very good. Nowadays, because of a more complex attitude, and the passing of the Victorian ' master and man ' framework, good relationships in any business house demand skilled study and the cultivation of efficient liaison between employer and employees.

Employees' Welfare Association

The Salvation Army Assurance Society has had an Employees' Welfare Association since 1940, when the Society was evacuated to ' Rosehill ', near Reading. This was brought about largely by emergency conditions existing through the outbreak of war. The need for representative machinery for the general welfare of employees was accepted by the Society and the first committee of the Association was elected by the employees. Mr. Cecil J. Matthews, then as now in charge of the Society's investments, was chairman of the new association from its inception until 1949.

Employees at The Salvation Army Assurance Society's Chief Office outnumber the officers in ratio of about two to one, a preponderence which is likely to increase, so that it is absolutely essential that the Society can recruit and keep a happy and efficient staff. In modern times this has occasioned considerable rethinking on the part of those in authority. It had, for example, been accustomed to pay a man somewhat in accordance with his marital status. Nowadays it has been found necessary to give him a salary commensurate with his seniority, ability and grade. Whether or not he has a wife is irrelevant. This change is one of a number which has brought Salvation Army Assurance Society procedure into line with that obtaining among other assurance companies and in the business world generally.

Then there lingered on for many years the idea, quite widespread in another time, that Salvationists should be willing to give their daily toil at a ' cheap ' rate, ' for the good of the cause '. But in modern times this idea has proved to be unworkable for a number of reasons. It is of doubtful Christian validity and in practice did not operate for the good of the Army—cheap employees are liable to give ' cheap ' labour. It is found within reason that ' the rate for the job ' gives the best return: good workers deserve and require a proper pride. Inadequate remuneration tends to inhibit this. Now, when compared with life offices of similar size, it can be said that Salvation Army Assurance Society salaries and incentives are on average equal.

Three Salvation Army Assurance Society employees are on the Associated Headquarters Clerical Staff Pension Fund as Trustees, as are employees from other headquarters. Salaries within the various grades can be agreed within the Society itself, whilst promotion from one grade to another, with the adjustments in salaries that this entails, is dealt with by another board at International Headquarters, on which The Salvation Army Assurance Society is represented.

Both at Head Office, and out on ' the field ', where officers and employees work together, one might expect that invidious comparison would be made between their relative remuneration. No Salvation Army officer gets a salary as such; he has an allowance. But he knows from the first, or should do so, that when he puts his hand to the plough, in response to the call of God, monetary award is not thereafter a significant part of his life: his rewards are paid in a different currency.

Not all are called to this ministry, and its criteria of judgment cannot automatically be transferred. The Salvation Army assurance agent, who can gain a very good financial return for his labour, or a senior administrative ' lay ' worker at Head Office, who is given a good salary, sees nothing incongruous in the disparity between his remuneration and the allowance of an officer. After all, it's all in the Bible. One young Salvation Army Assurance Society employee, subjected to heavy pressure, was told, ' You will not get anywhere unless you become an officer.' This is not now necessarily true. Whereas the possibility of rising to administrative responsibility was at one time restricted to officers, the way is now open for employees of proved ability to take such positions.

As it is, many employees at The Salvation Army Assurance Society office testify that staff relationships are good, that grievances are listened to sympathetically and, where a just case is made out, dealt with expeditiously. It is by no means unknown for those who leave to ' improve their prospects ' to return to the Society having found that they did not better themselves, and they were glad to return ' home '.

Members of The Salvation Army Assurance Society Employees' Welfare Association have every right to feel that they are an essential and recognized part of the Society.

Association of Agents

The Association of Agents of The Salvation Army Assurance Society Limited came into being in Glasgow, in 1944. It represented a challenge to the Society and was looked at with extreme trepidation because, to put it mildly, anything savouring of a trade union within the Army is not traditional.

Yet this Association has worked harmoniously, mutually helpful within the Society for the past eighteen years. When, in 1949, terms of agreement were recognized by Commissioner Frank Dyer, then the Managing Director, his letter intimating this official recognition contained these words, ' I trust this new development will work out for the good of the Society, the agent and above all The Salvation Army.' That this hope has been fulfilled is now abundantly clear.

As with the Employees Welfare Association the birth pangs of the agents' group was brought about by war, when many agents were on war service and assurance working conditions were more or less disorganized. The first Annual General Meeting of the Association was held in Blackpool, in 1950, and one has been held annually since. The present President, Mr. Walter George Fowler, a responsible Salvationist local officer, long experienced in Salvation Army life assurance work, says of the Association, ' We are Salvationists and we act accordingly.'

Twice yearly the executives of the Association meet the Society's management at the Chief Office in London. At these gatherings it would be easy to visualize explosive situations arising, ending in deadlock and worse: the sort of thing that is sometimes the outcome of industrial negotiations elsewhere. Indeed in the early days of the Association some people did express the view that this would be bound to happen. When the Association was recognized by the Army as a negotiating body there was a shaking of heads and forebodings of disaster.

But in the eighteen years of its existence the twice-yearly meetings with the management have resulted in highly beneficial developments, both for agents and the Society. There are sometimes disagreements but, as one Association executive put it, ' nothing beyond hope '. Sometimes the agents yield; sometimes the management yield; sometimes there has to be a compromise. Everything is done with goodwill.

Both at Blackpool, for the Annual General Meeting, and at Chief Office, for the consultations with management, the word of prayer and the word from the Bible has its place. Management and agents are joined by one common bond— Salvationism. There may be straight talking and even disagreement but there is mutual respect and acceptance of Christian responsibility.

Most ' run of the mill ' negotiations today, with agents and the Society, are done at local level through the Superintendent or Divisional Manager. It is when these fail, when there is some real, or imagined anomaly or injustice that the Association of Agents is asked to intervene. There is a consistent history of common sense and sympathetic under-standing on the part of management in the Society toward these misunderstandings and difficulties. By far the vast majority of them are happily ironed out. The first printed statement of the Association, back in 1944, contained these words: ' The Association is non-union, preferring to deal with Chief Office as Salvationists.' This proviso operates happily and is highly effective. The President of the Association of Agents declares that conditions of work and remuneration within the Society ' compare favourably with other societies '. And he pays high tribute to the Managing Director, General Manager, and others with whom the Association negotiates. The agents' representatives do not go to Chief Office to ask for the moon but to get results—and in this they are successful. There are hard-headed business men on both sides of the table who recognize that they cannot always win; they don't expect to.

It is now recognized that the Salvationist who seeks better working conditions or salary or both is not to be regarded with the horror Oliver Twist encountered in the workhouse when he asked for more. On the contrary, it is found that the Association's assessment of competitive conditions in the life assurance world, and the wish to share in the profits from developments and advances, is a good thing all round, tending to benefit the Army as well as the agent concerned.

Officers of the Association consist of president and vice-president, treasurer, secretary, and a number of agents elected to the executive committee. The election takes place annually at the Annual General Meeting. Members pay a monthly subscription and each branch of the Association is empowered to nominate one of its members to serve on the executive committee.

Chapter
Twenty-seven

LOOKING TO THE FUTURE

By 1965 the life assurance market was affected by the 'squeeze', which asked not whether this or that society was run on religious or socially deserving lines, but pressed equally hard on all. There is always fierce competitive effort in maintaining a life assurance concern. Indeed, it is axiomatic that if a society is not making headway then it must be going back; it is not possible just to preserve a *status quo*. Many of the men who had been the backbone of the Society were growing older, passing on, retiring. They were of that 'special breed', the Founder's 'ordinands' and their direct descendants, men of that ilk whom Commissioner Albert Mingay recently described as 'the cream of Salvationist manpower in Scotland'. Replacing such men is no easy problem.

So there is a staff shortage. Perhaps there always has been, but it has varied with the economic condition of the country and the fluctuations of the spiritual climate of the Army. Willingness to sacrifice, ability to resist the lures of affluence, seem to vary from one generation to another. Yet the future of The Salvation Army Assurance Society must depend largely on its ability to attract manpower to carry out that tradition of personal service which should be the ideal aim of the Salvationist agent.

As Brigadier John Hansen is specially responsible for finding and training men for work in the Society, one might expect, in these days of manpower famine, to find him suffering from some degree of frustration and pessimism. But this would be wrong. This cheerful, optimistic and successful Candidates Secretary of The Salvation Army Assurance Society is finding new men who are as willing as were the pioneers to give themselves to this work. They feel it to be work for God.

'It must not be for money,' the Brigadier insists. 'The

heart must be in it. It is an opportunity to live a worthwhile life, to express one's religion through one's daily work.' Work, homelife and general background are thoroughly investigated prior to acceptance.

Training, eight weeks in residence at a training centre in London, includes accommodation for the family, if any. The programme may take in such elementary matters as letter-writing and accounts, but goes on to public relations and ' salesmanship ' of the Salvation Army brand. This concentrates for the most part on the qualities of mind and heart, the religious make-up of the man that must be the Salvation Army Assurance Society ambassador in the homes of the people.

There are certainly no offers of affluence. But it is not poverty either. One new man who recently joined the Society declared that he can give his wife more house-keeping money from his Superintendent's allowance than was the case in his pre-Salvation Army Assurance Society days. He was then earning £22 a week.

What the position of Superintendent gives is a job-plus, a proper pride. It is the present-day confirmation of the claim of William Booth that a man should go unashamed into people's homes collecting premiums on life assurance while all the time concerned in advancing the Kingdom of God. This is the reason new agents, employees, ' laymen ' superintendents and officers alike, have been found who would give their lives by a divine compulsion when other easier and more renumerative possibilities lay before them.

It is a future of attractive business possibilities as well as spiritual soundness. The man who wishes to develop the personal, regular weekly clientele in industrial branch life assurance can do so. He is likely to be a man with gifts of personality rather than professional assurance expertise. The man with a gift for modern-life office method may favour the quarterly or half-yearly premium and a larger proportion of better-off people in his clientele. Some can happily combine both methods of collecting premiums.

Brigadier Hansen certainly encourages his candidates

to take a large view of their options. ' It took us seventy years to produce £1,000,000 per annum from investments,' he says. ' But we shall double that in ten years. In the old days we could consider it an achievement to get a poor man's signature on a £20 proposal; now we can sell him an industrial policy for £1,000.'

' This is a career that extends a man,' he goes on. ' He can fulfil God's purpose for him yet live a full and happy life at the same time.' That is why there is nothing apologetic about Salvation Army Assurance Society advertising. This one, in *The War Cry* for example:

LET OTHERS SHARE THE GOOD NEWS!

It may seem a far cry from the gospel to life assurance but there is a connection. The Salvation Army Assurance Society offers security as good as any available today. More than this, policy-holders help to spread the gospel all over the world—and in The Salvation Army that means good news.

The Musician advertisements specifically aim at potential agents who are told that there is ' ample scope for promotion ' and the response, much of it from highly suitable people, shows that such advertising makes an impact. Among recent candidates for work as officers in The Salvation Army Assurance Society is a professional man (A.C.I.I.) and his wife who have been accepted for training at the International Training College at Denmark Hill. Another is a Post Office engineer who, with his wife, recently became a Salvationist. Both these men, and numerous others, have recently taken similar decisions in the belief, as Brigadier Hansen says, that it is ' something of the heart '—something more than money.

So, in the minds of those at ' the top ' in The Salvation Army Assurance Society, those oldest and most experienced, and those who are newly committing themselves to lifetime service in it, the Society has a future. It will be a ' different ' Society. While it holds to William Booth's vision it must be. Not for it the ' remote control ' revenue of the affluent investor, the depersonalized emphasis on profits alone that must be the chief concern of the ordinary commercial life office.

Like many of William Booth's ideas The Salvation Army Assurance Society is extraordinary. It genuinely seeks to provide a duality of purpose: life assurance as such, on competitive terms, and also a ministry of dedicated men and women who visit about 350,000 homes regularly and who are concerned not only about the premiums but the people who pay them. This was what the Founder felt in his heart when in 1912, the year he passed on and when nearly blind, he wrote to Carleton:

My dear Comrades,

Your General greets you!

Favoured with so capable, so devoted and so useful a Commissioner, possessing so anxious and so earnest a body of workers, inspired by so fervent a desire to promote the temporal and eternal benefit of the people who use it, and having already won so powerful a hold on public opinion, how can The Salvation Army Life Assurance Society be other than the striking success that God has already made it, and better still, which God is going to make it in the future?

To help you in accomplishing this desirable end is the determination of

Your affectionate General.

If he can see his Society now, doubtless he is content. It is what he felt it ought to be—a unique society.

ACKNOWLEDGMENTS

THE author gratefully acknowledges generous assistance from various sources which include: The Atlas Assurance Co., Ltd.; Britannic Assurance Co., Ltd.; The Equitable Life Assurance Society; General Accident Fire and Life Assurance Corporation, Ltd.; Guardian Assurance Co., Ltd.; Legal and General Assurance Society Ltd.; Liverpool Victoria Friendly Society; The London and Lancashire Insurance Co., Ltd.; Methodist Church Press and Information Service; Methodist Insurance Co., Ltd.; Norwich Union Insurance Group; Pearl Assurance Co., Ltd.; Prudential Assurance Co., Ltd.; Refuge Assurance Co., Ltd.; The Royal London Mutual Insurance Society, Ltd.; Royal Liver Friendly Society; Stone and Cox, Ltd.; Sun Alliance Insurance Group; Wesleyan and General Assurance Society.

Thanks are due, also, to Commissioner William A. Villeneuve, Managing Director of The Salvation Army Assurance Society, not only for making available maximum assistance within the Society but also for patience and kindness when delivery of the finished manuscript was delayed. Among others who rendered assistance were Colonel Frederick Grant, Lieut.-Colonel Leslie Martin, Mr. Cecil Hayday, Mr. A. Farncombe, F.I.A., of Bacon and Woodrow, Consulting Actuaries, Brigadier Charles Lambert, Mr. George Hurren and Colonel Railton Howard. I am also particularly grateful for the patient and skilled assistance of Brigadier John Martin, Editor of *Assurance*.

B. W.

INDEX